Edward Enfield

OLD AGE AND HOW TO SURVIVE IT

summersdale

OLD AGE AND HOW TO SURVIVE IT

Summersdale Publishers Ltd
46 West Street
Chichester
West Sussex
PO19 1RP
UK

www.summersdale.com

Printed and bound in Great Britain

ISBN: 978-1-84024-776-3

Edward Enfield

OLD AGE
(AND HOW TO
SURVIVE IT

Acknowledgement

Readers of *The Oldie* magazine may notice that in this book I have occasionally repeated some passages from the column which I write in that sparkling publication. I am grateful to Richard Ingrams, the editor, for agreeing that I may do this.

Contents

Old Age and How to Survive It

'I have no complaint to make against old age.'

Gorgias of Leontini (c.483–c.385 BC)

The phrase 'old age and how to survive it' must be some kind of figure of speech, but I am not sure what. It is not quite an oxymoron, but it is getting on that way. An oxymoron, according to *The Chambers Dictionary*, is a figure of speech in which contradictory terms are combined, such as 'falsely true' or 'bitter sweet' and other things along

those lines. That does not seem exactly to cover the matter of survival of old age, and I have looked through *Kennedy's Latin Primer*, which great work has a copious appendix of figures of speech, many with lovely names such as 'hysteron-proteron' or 'hendiadys', but none of them describe a phrase which seems to be sense but is actually nonsense. Perhaps it is a non sequitur, or even a contradiction in terms, but perhaps not, and perhaps I have invented something new.

The plain fact is that nobody since the days of Adam and Eve has ever survived old age, and nobody ever will as it always gets you in the end. People use the phrase 'as old as Methuselah' and according to the book of Genesis 'all the days of Methuselah were nine hundred sixty and nine years'. It then adds 'and he died' which must have

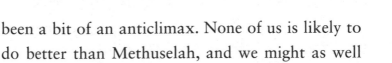
been a bit of an anticlimax. None of us is likely to do better than Methuselah, and we might as well get used to the idea.

The word 'survive' is used, however, in another sense. People write articles in newspapers headed 'How to survive Christmas' without there being the least suggestion that their readers are likely to drop dead if they don't take care. In that sense I have no difficulty at all in surviving old age as I like it very much. I like it better than youth or middle age, and this is, indeed, my only qualification for writing this book. I am not a psychiatrist, a psychiatric social worker, hypnotherapist or author of self-help books with enticing titles such as *How to Make a Million Pounds in 48 Hours*. All I am is old.

I was born on 3 September 1929, which is a long time ago, and as I look at this date I have a very slight twinge of regret. Fairly recently the government decided that those who had made a contribution to winning the last war should be rewarded by having their passports renewed free of all cost. It seemed to me to be a strange gesture, but nevertheless a generally benevolent one. You were not required to prove that you had helped to win the war, you just had to have been alive for at least ten years before it started. As the war started on my tenth birthday, 3 September 1939, I missed out by a matter of hours, and while I cannot see that I helped the war effort in any way at all, I should have liked to have been included among those who did. However, as my passport will not need to be renewed until I am eighty-two years old, I think this may not matter very much. As everyone who qualifies is, by definition, even older than me, I suspect that this stroke of generosity may not have cost the Chancellor a great deal. Most of the beneficiaries will be too old to leave the country anyway so it is a sort of reverse stealth tax, a benefit which is announced with much publicity and is of use to very few.

But that is by the way. The great Roman orator and philosopher Cicero remarked that old age is a strange business. No one wants to miss it, he said, and everyone complains about it when they get there. Not I, though. Take it from me that the best thing to do about old age is to enter on it at the first possible opportunity, so that you have time to enjoy it properly. There was indeed a Latin proverb: 'You must be old soon if you would be old long' (*Mature fieri senem, si diu velis esse senex*). With this I most heartily agree.

The Electrician's Mate's Syndrome and Its Fearful Dangers

'Leisure is the great comfort of old age.'
Marcus Tullius Cicero (106–43 BC)

The best preparation for a glorious retirement is to be a wage slave in an office or factory. This gives an added relish to the exciting moment when you can leave off going to work, which is something on which people in other walks of life may easily miss out. Actors, it seems to me, have a strange addiction to having people clap them. They like to stand on the stage at the end of a play and be clapped, and then to walk off in order to walk back on again so that they can be clapped some more. Once you are hooked on that sort of thing it is obviously difficult to manage without it, which is why they tend to keep going, or to keep going on and off, until it is obvious to everyone but themselves that they are past it. Thus again, if you are a steeplechase jockey, you may be quite put out when you have to give up riding, as you would much rather carry on if only you hadn't got too fat or broken too many bones. It is not like that for us office workers, or at least, it should not be.

The day of retirement comes. A body of people assembles, and at least one speech is made, of which the general drift is that you are one of the finest fellows going, and they will be hard pressed to manage without you. They may well give you a present, which by tradition used to be a clock but in my case was a tent. They gave me a tent to take with me when I cycled across France, which is just the sort of thing you ought to do when you retire, as I will explain in its proper place. Having been

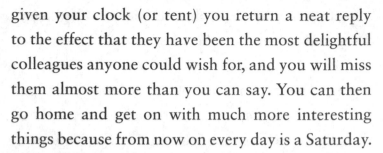

given your clock (or tent) you return a neat reply to the effect that they have been the most delightful colleagues anyone could wish for, and you will miss them almost more than you can say. You can then go home and get on with much more interesting things because from now on every day is a Saturday.

I don't know that I am a particularly lazy man, but I always liked the weekends better than the weeks, and preferred being on holiday to going to work. It is not always so, which is where the electrician's mate's syndrome comes in. I can warn you of its dangers by adapting a little rhyme of C. S. Calverly:

> 'People with this disease
> Become by slow degrees
> Brainless as chimpanzees
> Meagre as lizards.
> Go mad and beat their wives,
> Plunge, after shocking lives
> Razors and carving knives
> Into their gizzards.'

An electrician commonly works with a mate. The mate is junior in status and, I assume, carries the bag, fetches the tools and runs up and down stairs or in and out to the van. For many years the electrician is waited on in this way and then suddenly when he retires, the mate is gone. Being now in a lonely state he looks around for a substitute and casts his wife in the role of mate, expecting her to hang around after him all the time, in the same submissive way. She, poor woman, has been used to having him out of the house for at least five days a week, and has been dreading his retirement anyway. 'A man is *so* in the way in the house,' says one of the ladies of Cranford, and here he is about the place with nothing to do and expecting her to dance attendance on him all the time. The outcome is likely to be disaster and the condition may be fatal, as the rhyme that I quoted indicates.

The worst case of EMS that I

have come across concerned a man who was not an electrician but a local government officer. He was in a senior position, and everyone else in the department had to attend the frequent meetings that he called and, once there, to listen to what he had to say. He also had a secretary who used to fuss over him like a demented parrot. Most secretaries fuss over their bosses a bit, but she fussed more than most and this is a most dangerous thing. There is an early state of EMS called My Secretitis, of which the symptom is that the patient keeps talking about a character called My Secretary. I once was walking behind a man and his son-in-law, and overheard the father-in-law say to the son-in-law: 'We must have lunch. Get your secretary to ring my secretary.' Anyone who says that instead of 'give me a ring' is in a fair way to getting EMS.

The man whom I have in mind as seriously afflicted with EMS had a plan to ease the pain of retirement, which was to set up a consultancy. The closer the day of retirement came the more he talked about his consultancy, and the enormous tax advantages he would reap from it, and how he would never again pay for a foreign holiday but would charge all the costs as business expenses to be funded somehow by the Inland Revenue. When the time came, he went, he formed his consultancy, and found that nobody wanted to consult him about anything. There was no matter on which anyone needed his help and no subject on which his opinion was thought to be worth paying for. This was bad, but there was no screeching secretary to attend to his wants and minister to his self-esteem and this, I suspect, was probably even worse. I think it kindest to draw a veil over what followed, and just to say that it was all too much for him.

To avoid such terrible risks you must realise that retiring is something like drowning. There is a brief disturbance of the surface, but when you disappear from sight the waters close over the place where you once were, and everything flows on as before. Whatever flattering remarks they may make when you leave, do not believe for a moment that you are anything other than completely dispensable. Sydney Smith, the eighteenth-century clergyman, put it that 'Few men have the good sense to realise that they must inevitably be forgotten, or the fortitude to bear it when they are.' The phrase is unfortunately too long to inscribe on a gold watch but it would make a salutary inscription on a silver tankard.

The agreeable side of being absolutely unwanted is that you are positively free, and the time to cultivate the delicious feeling that this inspires is in bed, first thing in the morning. For years, perhaps for eight or ten years after I retired, I used to wake up with a cosy warm glow of happiness. 'Why am I so pleased?' I would wonder drowsily, and then it would come to me: 'It is because I haven't got to go to work. Not today, not tomorrow, not ever.' Sometimes this wholly delicious sensation was given an added piquancy by my dreaming, immediately before I woke, that I was still at work and harassed by the sort of difficulty that one gets in dreams (and sometimes in life). I might, in my dream, have been sent at short notice to address a committee on a subject about which I knew nothing, or have been holding up some important proceedings while I searched desperately for a missing set of papers. Then I would snap awake and find, to my enormous pleasure, that all that sort of thing is in the past. 'With a bound, he was free' is a phrase of which the writers of penny dreadfuls were supposed to be fond, and it exactly describes my feelings on waking from a dream of local government. Unfortunately, with the passage of time, this wears off. It is now some sixteen years since I did anything which could seriously be called work, and the idea that my time is entirely my own is no longer the exciting novelty that it was at first. Meanwhile, I can tell you that the place to find people with a proper view of the prospect of retirement is on commuter trains, where there are always a great many people who are looking forward eagerly to the day when they do not have to commute on commuter trains any more.

On the Declining Years, with Some Observations on the Centurion in the Bible

'It is better to be at leisure than to be busy about nothing.'

Pliny the Younger (AD 61–113)

I had a friend and colleague who, as is the way of things, retired. Three months later he came back to visit me in my office, springing in on the balls of his feet and looking ten years younger.

'Hello Len,' said I. 'How are you getting along?'

He bent his head close to mine and said in a confidential tone, 'I have discovered the secret of happiness.'

'Quick!' I said. 'Tell me at once – I need to know.'

'It is doing the things you want to do,' he said, and then he paused before adding the vital words, '*and not doing the things you don't want to do.*' Then he nodded, much in the manner of a wise owl, and, as far as I recall, bounced off with springy steps.

This secret is far more important than that of the philosopher's stone, which was supposed merely to tell you how to turn things to gold – and gold, as is well known, is not the key to happiness, though it can help.

My own contribution to philosophy has been to develop a theory of the Three Ages of Man. The first period, which lasts for about twenty years, could possibly be called the Conjugating Years, this being the period in which I, at least, and many others learnt the skill of conjugating verbs in foreign languages. It could equally well be called the Declining Years because you also learn to decline foreign nouns and adjectives, but this would lead to confusion with a later period.

The next age is that of the Accepting Years. This lasts for about forty years, and is so-called because you have to accept a great many things that you would rather not, such as the need to go to work, or invitations from people you don't care for. It is neatly expressed by the Centurion in the gospel of St Matthew, who remarked, 'I say to this man Go, and he goeth; and to another Come and he cometh, and to my servant, Do this and he doeth it.' There they all were, hopelessly caught up in a tangle of accepting orders to Go when they would probably rather Stay; to Come when they might to prefer to Remain Where They Were and

Finish Their Card Game; and to Do this when they would much rather Do something quite different. This accepting is a tedious business, but it gives a spice to the third period, that of the Declining Years.

This is the period in which you decline to do anything you don't feel like doing, and is therefore much the best. As well as declining to listen to the conversation of people whose opinions you do not think worth having, you very rarely need to move in any direction or at any time that does not absolutely chime in with your own inclinations. You need only to be on your guard against well-intentioned but misguided people who try to march you down to the local comprehensive school and enrol you in woodworking classes in order that you should 'do something'. This amounts to Age Harassment and should be made a criminal offence.

One of the great delights of the Declining Years is that the list of things you don't have to do is constantly expanding. You do not have to take your children to Disneyland because they are too old and you do not have to take your grandchildren to Madame Tussauds because that is a job for their parents. These, to me, are wonderful thoughts and it is such comfortable reflections that give a special zest to the pleasures of the Third Age.

On Not Wanting Things in General, but Odd Things Occasionally

'The rich never want anything very hard
except maybe someone else's wife.'

Raymond Chandler (1888–1959), *The Long Goodbye*

Shortly before I stopped going to work I read somewhere that this was the moment when I should go out and buy all the things I wanted because I wouldn't be able to afford them when I had retired. I pass this on as a valuable piece of advice, as it is a cast iron excuse for a spending spree and enables you to commit all sorts of extravagances with an absolutely clear conscience. I bought, for myself, a new bicycle and a radio and I would like to think I bought something for my wife but it is so long ago that I cannot remember. I may possibly have bought her an electric typewriter, which is not a very exciting present, but it could be that she had already got ahead of me and didn't want anything anyway, except for that.

With luck, you will find that this piece of advice, although enjoyable when you put it into practice, is wrong twice over. You may find that you are perfectly able to afford all the things that you want, and this may well be because you don't want very much anyway. Indeed, one of the pleasures of getting older and older is that you care less and less about more and more. I never wanted a Lagonda, a Rolex watch, a yacht or a racehorse, and now I have an enormous list of all the other things I have no wish for. I do not want to go line dancing or on a cruise, because I am too unsociable; I do not want a holiday in Barbados, because we have had one, and one is enough. I do not want to dress myself up in the ridiculous clothes that are worn by male models in advertisements, and I do not want a holiday home in the Dordogne, as the Dordogne is too far away and one house is enough to manage. Going without things that I do not want has become a constant source of virtuous entertainment, and if I were a reformed alcoholic I should spend a lot of time looking in the windows of off-licences to enjoy the sight of the stuff by which I am no longer tempted. I remember spending an enjoyable time at Victoria Station wandering through the shops looking at all the things I had no wish to buy. It became a sort of litany: 'I do not want any patterned socks. I do not want any jockey briefs.' Then I turned into WHSmith. 'I do not want *Farmers Weekly*. I do not want *Autocar*. I do not want *Women's Writing* and I do not want Black and Gay Literature.' I found it a most peaceful and innocent way of passing the time.

And yet, I have to confess, every now and again something turns up which I do rather want, and it is almost bound to be an old book. Within the last two years I have bought two very expensive books, one being the Foulis Press edition of Homer (1756) and the other being William Martin Leake's *Travels in the Morea* (1830). They are both in excellent condition and beautifully bound, and as well as the pleasure of reading them I have the certainty that if I were a multimillionaire collector not only would I like to have these books but also, however rich I was, I could not possibly have better copies. Edward Gibbon, author of *The Decline and Fall of the Roman Empire*, said that he did not know why it was but he got greater pleasure from reading Homer in this edition than in any other, and I agree. William Martin Leake is one of my heroes, a royal engineer officer who, somehow, but no one is sure quite how, turned himself into the greatest authority on the topography of classical Greece in modern times, and this is the first edition of one of his most important works. Now, both of these purchases were simple extravagances on my part. I was not looking for these books, I was not pining to possess them, they just turned up. If I had not been able to strike an acceptable bargain with the bookseller for the one, or had been outbid at auction for the other, I could have managed quite calmly to have done without them, but an occasional extravagance of this sort is an undoubted pleasure and not inconsistent with the general enjoyment of not wanting a huge range of things that other people do want.

Having said that these were extravagances, on the subject of extravagance I will tell you about an American lady called Mrs Stevens. In the years after the war my father used to go pretty regularly to America on the *Queen Mary*, and on one of his trips he met and, rather to my mother's surprise, brought home this Mrs Stevens. She had come to buy antiques, and she stayed in our house in Sussex for about a week, making forays into antique shops and ordering grandfather clocks and card tables to be packed up and shipped off to the USA. I liked her, and she sent me some socks when she got home again, but I remember her chiefly for her dictum that '*You often regret your economies but never your extravagances.*' This I have found to be entirely true. There are one or two things I can think of that I dithered over and wish that I had had the courage to buy, but nothing that I have splashed out on that I regret.

Thinking of Mrs Stevens has reminded me of antiques, and antique shops are like the shops at

Victoria Station: full of things that I do not want. The pleasure I get from not wanting them is much enhanced by the fact that they often cost a great deal of money. People like me are known in the trade as time-wasters, this being the technical term that those in the antique business apply to those who have no intention of parting with money. This is a derogatory term, and relegates people like me to a sort of second rate status, which I can tell you how to avoid. You must think of something, or preferably two things, which the shop owner is most unlikely to have, and then ask if he or she has got it or them. On this basis, I have had, over and over again, conversations like this:

Antique dealer: Can I help you?

Me: Yes. I am looking for a bust of Homer. Do you have such a thing?

Dealer: No, I am afraid not.

Me: Or a bust of Vergil. Either would do.

Dealer: No, at present, I haven't.

Me: Ah well – never mind. Is it all right if I look around?

Dealer: Of course.

By this ploy you have gained two advantages. You are to all appearances a person whose pockets are bulging with ready money which you are anxious to hand over in exchange for the right things. You have also gained the upper hand over the dealer by exposing a deficiency in his shop, much as if you had walked into a baker's shop and asked for currant buns and they hadn't got any. You can now freely browse among all the things that you have no intention whatever of buying, having earned a degree of respect from the owner. Once, though, the conversation went like this:

Me: Have you got a bust of Homer?

Dealer: Yes, there is one in the window.

So there was – a little bronze bust about five and a half inches high, said to be eighteenth-century, and made by the Lost Wax Method, whatever that may be. It was priced at £75 so I bought it with pleasure and like it very much. You can get some desirable items as long as you start by not wanting them and as I do not want two busts of Homer I have adjusted my technique in antique shops. I now ask if they have a bust of Vergil, or failing that of Cicero, and they never have – so far.

On Health

'Twenty years ago I knew a man called Jiggins, who had the Health Habit. He used to take a cold plunge every morning. He said it opened his pores. After it he took a hot sponge. He said it closed the pores. He got so that he could open and shut his pores at will.'

Stephen Leacock (1869–1944),
'How to Live to be 200', in *Literary Lapses*

It is very surprising to me that anyone is ill with anything any more because almost daily the newspaper has at least one story about some fresh breakthrough which is going to put paid to yet another disease. Things are usually in the early stages, but the people who have done the breaking through are confident, or at least hopeful, that in a few years they will have that particular illness altogether defeated, and you would think from the way they talk that there were not enough diseases left to absorb all the cures.

Today, on the very morning on which I wrote this, *The Daily Telegraph* told us that a pint of beetroot juice had been found to lower the blood pressure like anything. They had discovered this at St Bartholomew's Hospital, but that was about all the paper told you. I wondered whether the people at Barts had tried the juice of other roots but found that they were no use. Was parsnip juice a failure and turnip juice a washout? Beetroot juice had come up trumps in the matter of blood pressure, but did they try it for other things, and find that it was no help in treating chilblains or athlete's foot? Still, it was good for blood pressure, but the paper gave no clue as to how to make, or where to buy, beetroot juice, although you would think that such an exciting discovery would lead to a huge increase in the acreage of beetroot, to supermarket shelves being piled high with beetroot juice, and everyone with a touch of high blood pressure swilling the stuff down at the rate of almost a gallon a week. Somehow I do not think that this will happen. I expect that the humble beetroot, having had its moment of notoriety and excitement, will sink back into obscurity and be overshadowed by the next breakthrough tomorrow, to be followed by the next one on the day after that.

I will not give you any advice about health, as such advice as I might give is the sort you do not need. You do not need me to tell you that it is a good idea to take plenty of exercise. I read somewhere that the ideal arrangement for old age is to have a large area of lawn to mow, a good length of hedge to cut and plenty of stairs to climb. I am fortunate enough to have all that, but I have contracted out the hedge cutting. To balance that off, I have my study on the first floor so that I go up and down a dozen stairs innumerable times a day. Similarly, you do not need me to tell you to eat sensibly as the newspapers keep telling us that all the time. Likewise, I do not need to tell you to drink moderately, partly because the newspapers keep going on about that as well, but mainly because binge drinking is a sign of youth and immaturity, and not a weakness of old age. A bottle of wine holds six glasses, and for my wife and me such a bottle does two meals, with my wife drinking slightly more than one glass each evening, and I drinking slightly less than two. Now and again we vary it with some other kind of drink, but I think the alcohol consumption is much the same. This constitutes a simple pleasure and is either mildly good for us or slightly bad for us, depending on what the papers have to say on that particular day.

I will tell you, though, that I have made a mistake, which I tell you so that you can avoid it. I failed to insure my teeth. In the course of nature your hearing fades, your eyes get weak and your teeth give trouble. The benevolent National Health Service will give you a hearing aid and attend to your eyes, though you have to pay for your glasses, but in respect of your teeth you are on your own, National Health dentistry having been abolished by stealth throughout most of the country. I was given the chance to insure my teeth at a premium of £15 per month, but up to that time I had not spent anything like £180 a year on my teeth, so I spurned the offer. Within a year or two the rot set in and I have spent far more than that on keeping my mouth in working order, but nobody now would want to insure me. Once you hit sixty-five and start to draw the old age pension, you would probably be wise, if you can, to spend some of it on tooth insurance.

Otherwise, the principal worry that I have about my health is that if I started to take an interest in it I should probably make myself ill. On this basis I try to ignore it unless it forces itself upon my attention. Some people have medical dictionaries on their bookshelves in which they like to look up different diseases to see if they have got them. This is unwise. Others search the Internet for complaints to match their symptoms, which is a good reason for not having a computer in the house. As far as possible, as I have said, I leave my health alone.

I am, let it be said, very lucky, and I would add 'touch wood' except that I was cured of touching wood by a very devout girl from Northern Ireland. 'Touch wood,' I said, and was stretching out my hand for that purpose, when she said, 'There's no need to touch wood, Edward. The Almighty has it in hand.' I could see that His purposes were not likely to be altered by my touching a piece of wood, so I have given the practice up, and do not suppose that my temerity in saying that I am lucky enough to be in good health will lead Him to give me a heart attack in order to teach me a lesson.

Which being so, I try not to go to the doctor unless I have three things wrong with me at the same time. As the first thing has usually got better by the time I get the third thing it is quite rare for me to go at all. This is a pity in a way, as our doctors are so extremely nice that it is always a pleasure to visit them.

I went once with a bloodshot eye. 'You have broken a blood vessel,' said the excellent Dr Jeffrey. 'What we do now is take your blood pressure. Your blood pressure has nothing at all to do with it, but it is part of the medical mumbo-jumbo that I should take it, so I will.' Accordingly he strapped a bandage onto my arm, squeezed away at a rubber bulb, and after a bit said, 'There! I knew it. Your blood pressure is perfectly normal. Just wait, and your eye will get better.' Which of course it did, leaving me with a high opinion of his straightforward no-nonsense approach to doctoring.

Some years later I limped into the surgery with a sore toe. Dr Jeffrey had retired, but a friendly new doctor looked at my foot and said, 'It might be gout and it might not, but it doesn't make much difference. I will give you some pills which will make it better.' In twenty-four hours my toe hardly hurt at all, and in forty-eight I was cured. It is so rare to find anyone so thoroughly on top of the job, or any device that works as well as those pills, that I found it a most refreshing and encouraging experience.

A good many years after that the pseudo-gout came back, and this time I saw a young lady doctor who sent my blood pressure up. She gave me some more of the infallible pills, but noticed from her computer screen that no one had taken my blood pressure for seven years so she thought she had better do it, and it was up a bit. 'I will get the nurse to take it again,' she said. 'Nurses have a way of getting blood pressure down,' – and sure enough, my blood pressure when taken by a nurse went back to normal. From this you will reach the correct conclusion that there is a young lady doctor in our surgery who is so sweet and attractive that she is able to send up the blood pressure of an old chap like me, and it is worth being ill now and again for the pleasure of going to see her.

I must, though, come clean and admit to a degree of hypochondria in respect of the common cold. I hate getting a cold. A bad cold can upset your arrangements altogether, cause you to pull out of luncheon engagements or go through with them while feeling rotten, and cause you other annoyances of a similar nature. Therefore, if I feel one coming on I resort to everything I can think of which includes echinacea, vitamin C and ivy-thyme mixture. From time to time I read in the paper that, unlike beetroot juice, none of this works, but quite often I have felt, or imagined, a cold coming on, and after I blitz it with all three of these things it goes away. Also, my wife and I each eat two Brazil nuts every day. We do this because we met a lady from New Zealand who told us that two Brazil nuts a day help ward off Alzheimer's disease. Brazil nuts are delicious, so it is no hardship to eat them, and for all we know they may be doing us some good.

In the matter of the health of your memory, I will tell you, for interest, that I read in the paper a supposedly beneficial exercise, which is to review in detail the events of the day as you lie in bed just before you go to sleep. Beneficial or not, I find that it is quite pleasant to lie snugly there and think over whatever has happened from the moment you got out of bed that morning until you got into it again that night. An interesting aspect is that the great Cicero, in his work entitled *On Old Age*, puts into the mouth of the also great Marcus Porcius Cato these words: 'In order to exercise my memory, I practise the advice of the Pythagorean philosophers, by recalling to my mind every night all that I have said, or done, or heard the preceding day.' Whether or not it actually helps the memory, the idea has

at least got the merit of antiquity, which lends it a certain respectability, and this is a great deal more than can be said for most of what you read in the paper, including the bits about beetroot juice.

Lapses of memory can be unfortunate. Not long ago I was standing in the queue in the post office, as one does, when a youngish and attractive woman came and stood behind me.

'Hello,' she said, 'How are you? I haven't seen you for a long time.'

'Fine,' I said. 'How are you?'

'Fine,' she said.

While this spirited exchange was going on, I was thinking to myself, 'I know you. I know exactly who you are. I cannot think of your name, but never mind, I am sure I know you very well and I consider you to be very nice.' On the strength of this I said, 'I think you and I are on kissing terms, aren't we?'

At this, she offered me her cheek, and I kissed it. Then we chatted on, and from something she said I realised that she was not the person I thought she was – in fact she was someone entirely different whom I did not know at all well, and whom I had no business to be kissing in a public place, such as a post office queue. Luckily for me, she didn't seem to mind but I realised that I had been living dangerously. In fact, if you read that I have been arrested for molesting women in the street, you might as well believe it as it is quite likely to be true, though it will have been done with the most innocent of intentions.

As well as doing what you can for your memory, I would advise you not to struggle against deafness but to surrender to it, and get a hearing aid. Before either my wife or I had grasped the idea that we were getting deaf, we used to do the crossword together like this:

Wife, reading out the clue: Ready to bat but not opening, as seemed reasonable. Five and two.

Me: What?

Wife: Ready to bat but not opening, as seemed reasonable. Five and two.

Me: As seemed what?

Wife: What?

Me: What are the last words?

Wife: As seemed reasonable.

Me: Added up.

Wife: What?

Me: Added up.

Wife: Why?

Me: It is 'padded up' without the opening letter.

Eventually I tumbled to the idea that I needed a hearing aid, and so I went through all the tests and was fitted with a digital National Health model. I brought it home, put it in my ear, switched it on, and four and twenty blackbirds all began to sing, or so it seemed. Apparently they had been singing all summer and I had known nothing about it.

My wife was still holding out, and went on the theory that I could not hear her because I was deaf, but she could not hear me because I mumble. I felt that I had the support of the telephone in this matter, because I could often hear the telephone when she did not, and the telephone does not mumble but sends out a high note such as deaf people are apt not to hear. I was, I thought, close to persuading her but the telephone intervened again. We read in the newspaper of some hearing test which could be done down the telephone, so both of us did it. We were each of us, in turn, congratulated on taking the test by an effusive recorded Irishman. He then handed us on in turn to a recorded female 'expert' who pronounced three different numbers at a time against a background of hissing noises, while we pegged them back to her. After five minutes of this she told each of us that our hearing was 'within the normal range'. This my wife took to mean 'normal' but I said that the recorded female had asked me how old I was so 'within the normal range' might mean a bit deaf, like most old chaps of seventy-six, as I was at the time. After that we both did it again, my wife passing herself off as fifty, and I declared myself to be forty, which made not the slightest difference to either the Irishman or the female

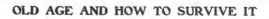

expert, as we were both still said to be 'within the normal range'.

That did us no good at all, but eventually my wife was persuaded to go for a proper test and was immediately offered a hearing aid, or two if she liked. She settled for one, and is still waiting for it, but when it comes I expect that she will get a surprise from the blackbirds and I shall mumble no longer.

On Being Oneself

'I have often wondered how it is that every man loves himself more than all the rest of men, and yet sets less value on his own opinion of himself than on the opinions of others.'

Marcus Aurelius (AD 121–180)

I went, not long ago, to a funeral, and a very good funeral it was, funerals being one of the very few things that have got better in my lifetime. They used to be solemn and melancholy occasions, but now they have got to be quite jolly affairs, with jokes about the deceased and a bit of a party afterwards. In this case I enjoyed the party most especially because there was a man there whom I particularly dislike, and so I had the added pleasure of not speaking to him.

I do not like this fellow because he is one of the most grubby-minded men I have ever met, and he fancies himself as a wit, but his attempts at humour are generally obscene, which is to me an adequate reason for not speaking to him. In fact it is a pleasure to avoid such a person altogether.

At one point during this funeral I saw the grubby-minded man sidling towards me, so I quickly sidled off on my own account and so escaped the need to exchange any words with him. I happened to tell another man that I did not like the grubby-minded man and he was rather distressed by this. He wished, and indeed offered, to effect a reconciliation between us, but I said I had no wish to be reconciled to a grubby-minded man whom I did not like, and any sort of conversation would quite destroy the pleasure I was getting from not speaking to him.

All of this I tell you as an illustration of one of the pleasures of old age, which is that you do not have to keep up a semblance of friendliness towards people whom you do not care for. This may seem to be, and indeed is, a negative advantage. On the positive side I am now much bolder than I used to be in such matters as confessing my ignorance without a blush. Some fifty years ago, when I was working in Bangkok, my wife and I were taken out to dinner by what used to be called a visiting fireman, otherwise a senior person from head office. 'We will start with smoked salmon,' he said, and then added, 'Now that I have chosen the first course, you must choose the second.' I was in the mood for steak; my wife is always in the mood for steak; I ran my eye down the menu, saw the words 'steak tartare' and ordered that. My wife, with a touching belief that I knew what I was doing, said she would have the same, and 'So,' said the fireman, 'will I.'

Now I certainly expected, and my wife equally certainly expected, and I do believe the fireman also expected, an ordinary steak with a tartare sauce but what came was a bloody pile of raw minced beef with a raw egg on top and a few capers on the side. My gorge rose at the sight of it, but I was far too shy to do anything other than pretend it was exactly what I wanted. My wife, rather than ruining my promising career, gamely went along with the pretence, and while the fireman went so far as to say he had forgotten that it looked quite like that, we all somehow forced it down our throats. It was the hardest dish I have every managed to make myself swallow, made worse by the knowledge that it had the makings of a perfectly delicious hamburger if only it was fried. If such a thing happened to me now, at the age of seventy-nine, I would simply say, 'I am terribly sorry – I had not realised that this was it. Please will you take it away and fry it?' If I had done that all those years ago my wife would have been most mightily impressed and the fireman possibly so relieved that he could well have promoted me on the spot.

I am also in my old age much bolder than I used to be in the matter of paying compliments to women. I think that this must be because I am now ready to risk looking foolish if the compliment falls flat, which is always a danger. In case it is of use to any elderly men who may chance to read these pages, my theory is that success lies not in the content but in the manner in which it is spoken. The words 'You are looking very elegant' or 'That really suits

you' may either produce a gratified 'Thank you' or
some variant of 'Do shut up you old fool.' I think
the trick is to make it sound utterly spontaneous,
as if it were wrung out of you by some irresistible
force. You could perhaps practise that in front of
a mirror, but anyway it is a great advantage of old
age that you can run such risks. From what I read,
if you tried it in what is called the workplace you
might well be done for sexual harassment, as the
line between a compliment and sexual harassment
is so fine as to be almost undetectable, so it is lucky
for me that I do not go to a workplace any more.

On Doing Less

'The years flowed on in a calm and we floated on in the stream of time towards the great ocean of eternity, like ducks and geese on the river's tide, that are carried down without being sensible of the speed of the current.'

John Galt (1779–1839), *Annals of the Parish*

When I think back, I am perfectly astonished at how much we used to do – or, to be strictly fair, how much my wife used to do. We have four children and so, at the peak, we constantly sat down six to a meal and sometimes more if there were visitors. She had all those meals to cook, and a house to run, and washing to wash, and school runs to manage, which you would think was enough, but it was far from all. There was always a dog to walk, and for a lot of the time there were ponies which needed things doing, such as having their heads held while the blacksmith saw to their feet. On top of all that, she would often drive twenty-five miles to visit her parents, and of all crazy things we used to have dinner parties. People used to arrive at a quarter to eight and go home abominably late, leaving us to wash up in the early morning hours before the rigours of the ensuing day. I will deal with the folly of such entertaining in another chapter.

I have a proper sympathy for housewives because I have some inkling of what it is like. I remember most clearly the time when I took ten days off from my work so that my wife could go to hospital to have the third baby. In a sort of way, I was managing the house and two children, though the task was made much easier than it would have been in real life because friendly neighbouring women kept turning up to give me stews and apple pies, as if I were some sort of earthquake victim. One day as I was driving the children to school I realised that my stomach was tied in a knot of desperate anxiety. 'I am terribly worried,' I thought, 'but I cannot think why.' Then it came to me – it was because I had not made the beds. I had devised a routine like this: get up; get washed; get dressed; get the children up; make the breakfast; make the beds; take the children to school – but on this day I had got behind schedule and missed out the bed making. Once it dawned on me that this terrible anxiety arose from such a trivial difficulty I was able to unwind the knot in my stomach and laugh it off. It taught me, though, that this sort of life is no easy matter, but rather a remorseless series of deadlines covering the whole day today and which will have to be encountered again tomorrow.

My own part in all this was comparatively meagre, but it was not nothing. I used to walk the dog before breakfast and then clear off to the office. When I got back I joined in the business of getting the children to bed, and my weekends were taken up with children, ponies, and a battle between me and the garden as to which should have the upper hand. A large part of my holidays seemed to be spent at the top of a ladder painting window frames and that sort of thing.

When all that goes away, you can begin to live your life in a civilised manner. Let me warn you against saying, 'I am now so busy that I don't know how I ever had time to go to work.' I urge you to avoid this, partly because it is a trite and tedious saying, and partly because it ought not to be true. To be comfortably occupied is one thing, but to be rushed and hurried is quite another, and shows a wanton disregard of your proper opportunities. You may not be rich in money, but you are rich in time, and ought to make the most of it. You will now have leisure, an inestimable gift, and its proper use is to let the simple pleasures of life expand to fill the time available.

Take, for example, the newspaper. Newspapers nowadays are full of terrible rubbish, but all the same breakfast never seems quite right without one. If we lived in a town I should take a daily stroll to the newsagent before breakfast to collect the paper, and I would do the same if we lived in a village. At least, I would were it not that the government now in power is set on destroying village post offices and these are likely to take the village shop and the village newsagent down with them in the general catastrophe. As things are at present, however, in our case the paper is delivered commendably early every day, and well before breakfast, by a man in a car.

In the old days, when I worked, I used to hurry through breakfast, take a quick look at the paper and dash off to the office. Not any more. We divide the paper in two, each of us reading our half in a leisurely manner and then we exchange bits and read the other half. Breakfast has lengthened to take about four times as long as it did before, and very pleasant it is.

Among all the stuff about footballers and celebrities there is a certain amount of news, and there are also columnists in great numbers. These freely offer their opinions on this and that, and after a bit you get to know whose opinions are worth having and whose are not (there being a great many of the latter). Also as a device to keep one's brain from seizing up they benevolently provide the crossword, sudoku, and recently some little mathematical puzzles as well. These are all good things. We do the crossword together as a team, and my wife does the sudoku and the maths puzzle by herself.

This is but the start of the day; the rest of it should, as far as possible, be conducted in a similar style. I cannot say that I have quite achieved it, but my aim is to get to something resembling the life of the master of a barge on the canals of Europe, as described in the late 1870s by Robert Louis Stevenson in a little book called *An Inland Voyage*. 'I am sure,' he says, 'I would rather be a bargee than occupy any position under heaven that required attendance at an office. There are few callings I should say where a man gives up less of his liberty in return for regular meals. The bargee is on shipboard; he is master of his own ship; he can land whenever he will, he can never be kept beating off a lee-shore a whole frosty night when the sheets are as hard as iron; and so far as I can make out, time stands as nearly still with him as is compatible with the return of bedtime or the dinner hour. It is not easy to see why a bargee should ever die.' Bearing in mind that we live in a house, which stays in the same place, rather than a barge, which moves, the bargee mentality is one that I try to cultivate.

On Not Wanting
a Computer

The people of Erewhon 'made a clean sweep
of all machinery that had not been in use
for more than 271 years (which period was
arrived at after a series of compromises), and
strictly forbade all further improvements
and inventions.'

Samuel Butler (1835–1902), *Erewhon*

The pleasure of not wanting a computer is
productive of so many other subsidiary
pleasures that it deserves a chapter on its own. It
is fruitful and multiplies, it produces shoots and

blossoms in the shape of yet other things that you do not want. If you do not want a computer, it follows that you do not want a printer, nor do you want broadband, whatever broadband is, nor yet do you want one of those cameras which takes pictures to be printed on a computer. People appear on the television to advertise wonderful things to do with computers that you can get at knock-down prices, and you can enjoy the thought of the money you have saved by not buying them, and then go out and spend it on something else.

The nearest I have come to dabbling in the new technology is to own a fax, which you will say is not very near at all, but I thought it pretty trendy at the time. Previously, when people wanted to send me something to read they used to say 'I'll fax it to you'.

'No,' I would reply, 'you can't do that. But if you put it in an envelope with a sticky bit of paper called a stamp, I will get it by nine o'clock tomorrow morning.'

They were generally quite surprised at this eccentric suggestion, but they humoured me, and it always worked. Then, as a concession to modernity,

we bought ourselves a fax, and almost at once they stopped saying 'I'll fax you' and began saying 'I'll email you' instead, which they can't, as I don't do emails.

You can, I am assured, do emails without a computer and you can have a computer without doing emails, but I do neither. I quite see that emailing is just the thing if you want to keep in touch with a sister in Australia, and I am constantly surprised by the number of people who have sisters in Australia, but as my sister only lives twelve miles away it is much easier just to ring her up. My eldest daughter, who is a dab hand at this sort of thing, travels the world and keeps in touch with her two daughters by email, or at least she tries to do so. Half the time they forget to collect, or download, or whatever it is you do to emails and so she arrives home unexpectedly because they have not found the email which she sent to say she was coming back. It may be that her messages get buried under a mountain of unsolicited pornography and electronic junk mail, which I am told is a feature of the business. Very recently I was talking to a man who said that after a week's holiday he had to spend half an hour pushing the Delete button on his computer to clear it of accumulated rubbish, and if I needed a reason not to have a computer, that would be enough.

I am not against owning a computer in principle, but my advice to any elderly person thinking of buying one would be 'Wait a little while and you will be able to get a better one'. I give this advice with complete confidence because I have followed it successfully myself ever since personal computers became available. During this time computers have been steadily improving and I have been patiently waiting for them to improve even more, secure in the knowledge that if I bought one today I should regret it tomorrow because by then they would have brought out a better one.

Computers and I go back a long way. I went to work at County Hall in Chichester in 1967, where the County Treasurer of the day had decided to go in for computer pioneering, and had bought one. It seemed to be a sort of monster, rather like the Minotaur in Greek mythology. I never saw it, but we understood that it was very big, and it had to be kept in a room with air conditioning and special ventilation to stop it getting too hot or clogged with dust. It was waited upon by a retinue of priests and acolytes called systems analysts and programmers who spoke a special language of their own and used to communicate with us in a sort of snuffle. I realise that this is a strange thing to say, but they all seemed to snuffle. They used to snuffle out computer jokes, saying things like 'Garbage In, Garbage Out' and then go off into a snuffling sort of laughter. There was one who used to come and say terrible things to me, such as 'I have now accumulated three man-years arrears of workload.'

The Minotaur which lived at the centre of a maze in Crete used to devour young men and maidens, and the computer lurked in its lair at County Hall and gobbled up public money. It had been bought as an economy measure, as it was supposed to do the work of many clerks at much less cost, at which it conspicuously failed. There was so much Garbage Out that the clerks were busier than ever, manually checking everything it did in order to detect the mistakes it made. County Hall itself became terribly overcrowded, and you could hardly open a cupboard without finding some computer expert inside, busily computing his arrears of workload. Nowadays all the people at County Hall have computer terminals on their desks and the air is thick with emails. No doubt things are better than they were, though when I left seventeen years ago there was still plenty of Garbage Out which they called Management Information.

You may say that computers can do wonderful things, and so they can. Young people understand them pretty well, and so do people in public offices and in public libraries, so you can always ask one of them to do it, whatever it is, if a computer is really needed. Otherwise, for us elderly people, not owning a computer is like not having a headache. It is something you are better off without and not to have one can be a positive pleasure.

I have kind friends who take an interest in my welfare and like to tell me how much I am missing by not having a computer, and how frightfully useful they find their own. They are, as I am able to point out to them, deluding themselves. What I am missing is a lot of aggravation. Those who have a computer at home spend much time, according to themselves, trying one thing after another to get some action out of the machine, followed by a lengthy call on the Helpline to some distant expert, and even in extreme cases sending for a friend who understands it all better than they do, to come and help out.

From all this I am free, but I am, I like to think, a fair man. I put the computer before you in this light, with the assurance that I myself manage very happily without one, so that you can weigh up the pros and cons before you give way to the undoubted pressure to conform, and go out and buy one. If you can find out how to manage it, then apparently lots of old people have a happy time surfing and social networking and that sort of thing, on a site called Saga Zone, set up by the admirable Saga organisation. It is, I read, 'A great place to share jokes and experiences with people of a similar age', and as so often in life, those that like it, like it a lot. On the other hand there is, in terms of a peaceful existence, a great deal to be said for keeping the new technology at bay.

On Money

'Remove far from me vanity and lies; give me neither poverty nor riches; feed me with food convenient for me.'

Proverbs 30:8

I am lucky enough never to have been seriously poor and so cannot speak of what it is like to be both poor and old. It does not take much imagination to see that it is unlikely to be pleasant, but all the same, I can think of one or two people who have very little money and yet appear to be as well satisfied with life as the rest of us. They have, I suppose, mastered the knack of being content with very little, '*contentus parvo*' in the Latin phrase, this being something of which the Romans very much approved, at least in theory. It would be foolish of me to pretend to know how this can be achieved, but I am full of admiration for those who manage it.

I have said that I have never been seriously poor but we have certainly been hard up, which we were for many years. My wife kept house on a very meagre budget, the children had presents of second-hand bicycles, but never new ones, and we just about managed one week's family holiday in a cottage in Cornwall – that is the way things were. We were members of what it has now become fashionable to call the Coping Classes. Then, gradually, things got better. My salary went up, the mortgage got paid off, we were left a little money, the children began to leave home, and we found we were quite comfortably off. The fact that we had once been hard up added to our enjoyment of this agreeable state of affairs.

It may seem egotistical to write like this about the Enfield family, but I do it only because there was nothing unusual about us. Most people are paid more when they are fifty than they were when they were thirty; mortgages do eventually get paid off; people do inherit little legacies and their children do begin to stand on their own feet. The question is: what happens when you retire altogether?

People have asked me, from time to time, how much money you need in order to live fairly comfortably in retirement. Until very recently I would have assured them that if they had belonged to a reasonable private or public pension scheme they may well find themselves to be richer than they have ever been before. We are constantly told of the huge 'pension pots' paid over to those in the public eye who have made a complete mess of things and been pushed into retirement, but there are many more people who have worked to the end and retired with much smaller pension pots with which they are very happy. These pots may amount to something like half pay, with perhaps a lump sum as well, and if both husband and wife have worked and are both in pension schemes, then there will be two pots, all of which is likely to come to a tidy sum, although I will not attempt to put a figure on it. The difficulty is that, as I write, we are trembling on the edge of a recession, if not a depression, and it is impossible to say how long this happy state of affairs can last.

Meanwhile, let us assume that you retire with something like half pay. On this you pay less tax than before, and you will not have to pay National Insurance contributions on your pension, and so you escape one of the more sinister of ex-Chancellor Brown's stealth taxes. Then, if or when you are sixty-five you begin to draw the old age pension and this has two effects. First your pension, plus the interest on your lump sum if any, plus the old age pension, with no NI contributions can add up to something close to what you had before. Furthermore, if you should happen to earn any money by any means whatever, they don't take NI contributions from any of it. Taken altogether you may get ahead of yourself and find that you now have more cash to splash about than when you worked full time. This is surely a tempting prospect, but there is more.

You will discover that, being old, you are assumed to be poor. As a group we are spoken of in company with those who earn very little. This government measure, or that rise in prices, will be particularly hard, they say, on the 'low-paid and the elderly'. They don't know what to do about the low-paid, but they shower gifts upon the elderly. The government gives us a Christmas present of £10. It assumes that we cannot pay our fuel bills, and so give us a couple of hundred towards that. They press free bus passes upon us, so that we can ride about on local buses for nothing, and they arrange for us to have cheap travel on trains. They give us free medicine, and they test our eyes for nothing. They reduce the price of entry to museums and such places, and this kindness extends to the continent of

Europe, where they eagerly ask you your age in the hope that they may be able to let you in at half price. At home, when we get to be seventy-five they give us free television licences, and when we get to be eighty, they increase our old age pension by 25p a week.

All this has produced the phenomenon known as the 'grey pound'. There has arisen a great army of pensioners who are rich in leisure and well off for money which they spend freely on things like holidays and cruises. Whole cruise ships are built to accommodate the grey pounders, and to take them to places like Venice or Dubrovnik where they go ashore in grey hordes to paint the town grey. The enormous success of the Saga organisation is based on persuading the grey people to part with their grey pounds on holidays like these.

It is, I fear, too good to last. By taking a sledgehammer to the finest pension arrangements in Europe and smashing them to bits, ex-Chancellor Brown has effectively spoiled things for those who come after us. In the course of time the cruise ships will either be laid up, sold to Disneyland or turned into prison hulks to accommodate the burgeoning community of criminals. Meanwhile we grey people should continue to make hay in the grey sunshine, with a virtuous feeling that by spending our money we are helping to support the economy.

On Being a Bore

'Old age is, by nature, pretty talkative.'
Marcus Tullius Cicero, *On Old Age*

I find that I am constantly told by young people to 'take care'. This is not, I think, due to any particular anxiety that I should wait for the green man to flash before I cross the road, or should keep a firm hold on the banisters when coming downstairs, it is just a general formula to usher me out of the door or bring a telephone conversation to a close. There are other ways of doing this, such as by saying 'see you soon' even though I may never see them again, or 'speak to you soon', although there is no reason to do any such thing.

I would, though, recommend you to take care in the matter of being a bore. We old people can be terrible bores, as was frequently pointed out to me by a young person of my acquaintance who was openly critical of the way some of the elderly behave. 'They go,' she said, 'to the post office at lunchtime. They have the whole day in which to go to the post office as they have long ceased to do any work or be anything other than a drain on the social services. Then, when they arrive at the counter they buy two stamps and make mad remarks to the person at the window, such as "I am eighty-two, you know."'

Yes indeed they do, and furthermore I think that some of us get our money out of the bank by asking the cashier for it instead of going to the cash dispenser, as there is no point in telling a cash dispenser that you are eighty-two but the cashiers have to listen. About a month ago I went to my bank to join a queue created by a plump, elderly lady in trousers who was leaning on the counter and blocking one of the two available windows. In a booming voice she was telling the unhappy girl

cashier, and incidentally the rest of us, that many years ago she had wanted to get a mortgage but was told that she couldn't have one because she was a married woman, and such people as married women were not allowed such things as mortgages in the days of which she spoke. There was, however, at that time a most ingenious manager of that particular branch who cleverly found a way round the difficulty by somehow granting her a loan which was in effect a mortgage in everything but name, but not a mortgage in fact, and so by means of this she was able to buy a house, for which she was extremely grateful. She wished, she said, to impress upon the cashier that the key to successful banking lay in finding a way to circumvent the rules in favour of the customers whenever such a thing was desirable, and this was something which she urged the cashier to bear constantly in mind in all her dealings with the bank's customers. Finally she heaved herself upright and said 'Well I mustn't keep you' much to the relief of the queue of twelve people that had built up while she was boring the cashier.

Now, while you need to avoid this sort of talk in public places or in talking to young people, among us old people such stories are the very stuff and substance of our conversation. I am sure that between ourselves the plump lady and I would have agreed that in our youth there were proper bank managers, sober and serious men with some experience of life who sat behind large wooden desks with leather tops and were to be treated with respect. We would have lamented the fact that nowadays bank managers can all too often be scrubby boys with sticky stuff on their hair whose desks are made of tin and plastic. Conversations such as the plump lady had with the cashier are boring to the young but interesting to the old because they tend to support the universal truth that things were better when we were young.

There is an everlasting argument between the generations on this point. We say that things were better in our youth, and they say that we only say this because we are old and old people always talk like this. We, of course, are right and they are wrong. We have a card in our hands which they can never hold, because we were there and they were not. We are speaking from first hand knowledge, whereas they can only speak of what they have read, or heard, or been led to believe by people as ill-informed as themselves.

As an example of the sort of thing the young quite misunderstand, I will take food and shopping in the days of rationing. They think that rationing must have been a great hardship, whereas it made shopping both simpler and more interesting than it now is. On the one hand you bought your ration and that was that. On the other, there were moments of excitement such as when the village grocer whispered to my mother 'I can let you have half a bottle of gin.' Gin was not rationed, you just couldn't get it, and so to come back from a shopping expedition having been slipped half a bottle in this way was a considerable triumph. I well remember the day when I was sent to do the shopping and came back with two lemons. Lemons had not been seen for years, so everyone got very excited, but nowadays you can buy all the gin and all the lemons that you want and there's no fun in it anymore. If I wanted to add a clincher to this argument I would remark that the nation was much better fed at that time than it is in the present age of rampant obesity, with cookery books and diet books jostling each other for first place in the best-seller lists.

An institution that has been comprehensively ruined in my lifetime is the University of Oxford, and while I cannot speak for Cambridge I expect that it has gone the same way. About Oxford I speak from knowledge. In my time we used to come into college hall for dinner wearing jackets, ties and gowns. The long Latin grace was spoken by a scholar who had to do it from memory and was not allowed to read it but was roundly jeered if he stumbled or had to be prompted. If you wanted a pint of beer you caught the eye of a college servant, called a scout, who brought it to you in a solid silver tankard. These tankards were all dated and I do believe they went back to the time of Charles II, the earlier ones having been melted down and the silver given to his father.

I can tell you what happens now, because I have been back and seen it. There are no jackets, ties or gowns, but the young people slope into the hall in any old jeans and T-shirts, looking awful regardless of gender (for half of them are now women). Scholars have been abolished, but someone now reads the grace in a halting manner from a printed card. There are no scouts anymore, and as it would be unwise to trust the modern undergraduate with a silver tankard, anything they want to drink (which is as likely to be Coca Cola as anything else) they carry in themselves from the cellar in the sort of glass mug that you get in public houses.

When I saw all this I felt sorry for the young people. A combination of a weak-kneed feeling by the college authorities that they could gratify the undergraduates by letting them be as scruffy as they like, with a mad zeal for expansion that has caused the college to outgrow its income and so be unable to afford scouts, has turned what was once a dignified occasion into an experience hardly more distinguished than eating in a works canteen. It has all been spoilt for the young, and when we old fellows get together we say to each other how lucky we were to have known it as it was. This sort of conversation we find to be intensely interesting, while to the young it is, of course, boring beyond words.

On Entertaining

'A feast was provided, at which we sate chearfully down; and what the conversation wanted in wit was made up in laughter.'

Oliver Goldsmith (1730–1774), *The Vicar of Wakefield*

It is some time now since we stopped inviting people to dinner, but there are those who have still not outgrown the habit, and I advise them to discontinue it at once, and ask their friends to lunch instead.

We reached this conclusion by degrees. In what I will call the old days, we could not ask people to lunch because there were children all over the place, and I was at my office during the week. Of necessity, therefore, we asked them to dinner, but they could not come until the children were out of the way, so they were told to arrive at 7.30 p.m. and turned up at about 7.45. We then sat about drinking till nearly 9.00, when we ate. After dinner there was more sitting around, some people drinking and some not, and as the clock advanced beyond midnight we would be hoping that someone would make a move towards going home, but with none of them wanting to be the first to break up the party. Eventually someone would mutter something about a busy day tomorrow, whereat everyone would discover that they all had busy days tomorrow, and depart, leaving us exhausted and, in my case, possibly hung-over.

As almost everyone else was in the same boat in respect of children, this was the universal way of things. We too arrived at their houses at 7.45 and got home after midnight. When I retired, I found that some people in their latter years were still carrying on like this from force of habit, but my eyes were opened to the possibility of doing otherwise by my former tutor at Oxford.

It will be obvious that anyone old enough to have been my tutor could not be a young man himself, and he made no bones about saying so. When he asked us to dinner he said 'Come at seven, as I like to go to bed early.' Accordingly we arrived at 7.00 p.m., the evening flew by, we left him at 10.00, and I woke next day feeling fit for anything. On thinking it over I could see that 7.00 was a good time to start the evening, but 6.30 would be even better. 6.30 is a perfectly sensible time at which to have a drink, 7.30 is a reasonable time to eat and 10.00 is an excellent time at which to go to bed. Accordingly I proposed that we should issue invitations on the lines of 'Come at 6.30 as we like to go to bed early', and I then included a little paragraph in my column in *The Oldie* magazine suggesting that other elderly people might like to do the same.

I found that the idea, though sound, is not infallible. A neighbouring lady, who had read my Oldie piece, being taken with the idea, tried it out. 'It was easy enough to get them to come at half past six,' she said, 'but not so easy to get them to go away. They were still here at midnight. In desperation my husband said, "Would you like to see the garden?" "Yes," they said, so he showed them round the garden, which he had to do by torchlight. When they came in, I felt I had to say, "Would you like a drink?" "Yes" they said. The only effect of your suggestion was that they were here for over an hour longer than they otherwise would have been.'

I had not thought of that difficulty, but being now aware of it we have given up evening entertaining altogether and only ask people to lunch. There is a lot to be said for lunch, in all sorts of ways. When I cast my mind back over a long life I can think of many more memorable lunches than I can dinners. I remember eating two large lunches in quick succession owing to a misunderstanding with my Chinese hosts, who had laid on a feast that I

had not expected, and which I had to eat although I had already eaten. For sheer splendour of food and circumstance, nothing could beat a lunch I was once given at the Worshipful Company of Vintners, though a lunch at the Café Procope in Paris runs it close. Lunch is how we keep in touch with friends and enjoy brief visits from the family. As well as all these merits, lunchtime entertaining has the great advantage that while it probably means forgoing your afternoon nap, it is a great deal better than being kept up until the early morning next day.

On Ending Up in a Pleasant Place

'I'm sick of portraits and wish very much
to take my Viol da Gamba and walk off
to some sweet village where I can paint
Landskips and enjoy the fag End of
Life in quietness and ease.'

Thomas Gainsborough (1727–1788),
in a letter to William Jackson

One of the things we old people do is give advice, and one of the things young people do is ignore it. I am currently giving very good advice to my grandchildren, and as they show not the least sign of taking any notice, I will repeat it here in case some other grandparent with more intelligent grandchildren may chance to read these pages. The advice is this: write letters, or visit, or get on the Internet, and by whichever means you prefer seek information from the Canadian, New Zealand and Australian High Commissions and perhaps the United States Embassy as well. Ask them to tell you which qualifications would make you an acceptable immigrant if you felt like emigrating. It will certainly be the case that some things on their lists will not appeal to you. There may, for all I know, be a great shortage of hairdressers in Australia and you may not like the idea of hairdressing (I can think of few things more unappealing than dealing with one head after another, day in and day out, especially in Australia). If you don't like it, you are not obliged to go in for it, but there might be some other subject which both seems to you a reasonable kind of profession and which is widely called for in the Antipodes or North America. Whatever it is, if they want it in the New World they will very likely want it in the Old as well, so you would not lose by qualifying in it, whether or not you choose to emigrate.

That may seem to be remote from the idea of old age, but it isn't, as it relates to the Roman idea set out in the Latin tag *'respice finem'* – 'look to the end'. It is hardly possible to start planning your old age too early, and therefore you should consider carefully, while still young, not only how you wish to spend your working life, but where you wish to spend your latter years, and how you are to support yourself in them. For many readers this will come too late, but I write partly for the benefit of irresponsible youth who regard old age as something which happens to others. I once thought that about marriage and about parenthood, both of which happened to me, although they are avoidable, unlike old age, which is not.

Another of my very best bits of advice, which I have never known anyone to follow, is 'get a job in a fire brigade'. This always takes them by surprise as they, whoever they are, have never thought of it, and I myself would never have thought of it, but for my inside knowledge gained in my years in local government. I am not sure that I would have followed it myself, but it is a particularly brilliant suggestion for any young person who aspires to be a writer or painter, or go in for some such chancy profession, which will not bring in much money to start with and may never bring in much at all, ever.

The great merit of the fire brigade is that the hours are concentrated, the retirement arrangements excellent, and brigades are to be found all over the country.

To take the hours first, firemen work a forty-two-hour week, being two nine-hour day shifts and two fifteen-hour night shifts, and then they have four days off. These two day shifts are spent, if there are no fires to fight or accidents to attend to, on training or, I suppose, polishing up the engine. The two night shifts are spent at the station waiting for something to happen, which waiting can be done, I imagine, while playing cards, or sleeping or more or less anything you may choose. As long as no fires break out or accidents happen it is much like being at home, except that you are at the station.

Now, should you be a fit and able-bodied young person, fresh from a Creative Writing course at the University of East Anglia with an eager desire to get on with your great unwritten novel, what could be better than the fire brigade? You have four whole days in every week in which to scribble away, and

I see no reason why you shouldn't scribble also on the night shift. A steady income keeps coming in and the rate of pay is by no means bad, with a whole ladder of promotion you might climb if you wanted to try. Your fellow firefighters will be supplementing this by cleaning windows and moonlighting in one way and another while you get on with your writing or painting or sculpting or pottery or whatever it is that you do. There are only two snags that I am aware of. There is a certain amount of danger in fire fighting, but it cannot be much, as not many firemen are killed each year. Also, cutting people out of grisly road accidents is something firemen do, and for this you must have a fairly strong stomach and not be one who faints at the sight of blood.

I have said that you should start on old age at the first opportunity, and of course the best way to do this is to make yourself frightfully rich. One way of getting frightfully rich is to write bestselling novels, and another is to create works of art which are bought by the likes of Charles Saatchi, for which you would have plenty of opportunity in your regular four days off. If, however, as is always possible, your works of fiction fail to sell and your daubs and collages fail to win the Turner Prize, then there is the comforting fact that the fire service pension scheme would give you one sixtieth of final pay for every year of service, which you can start to draw at the age of sixty.

The other enormous merit of fire brigades is that they exist, as I have said, all over the country. If you want to live in a busy city, then big cities always have fire brigades, and if you want to live in a country town, many country towns have fire stations. If you fancy living in a thatched cottage with roses rambling round the door, you may well

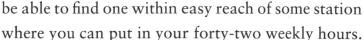

be able to find one within easy reach of some station where you can put in your forty-two weekly hours.

In having places of work all over the country the fire service is not alone. Being, as I am, a retired local government officer, I am very much alive to the fact that there are local government offices of one sort and another in every county in every big city. This offers enormous choice as to where you might live while you are working, and where you may be established when you come to retire. You might, for instance, have a hankering to live in the Lake District, but there are not too many ways of earning a living in that remote part. There is, though, an undeniable county council, and people are needed to work for it. Any reader with grandchildren would do them a great favour by putting this chapter before them and trying to persuade them to read it. In weighing up the prospects of the fire service and the opportunities in New Zealand they should consider also what qualifications might make them acceptable to local authorities in Cumbria. This, at least, would be a sound thing to do, but do not be disappointed if, being young, they take no notice of the suggestion.

On Not Doing Things Together

'Cato writes that Scipio Africanus used to say that he was never less alone than when alone.'

Marcus Tullius Cicero, *On the Republic*

If you are lucky enough to have a wife or husband when you retire (and I speak as a husband of over fifty years), then make an agreement either tacitly or explicitly that you will not do everything together. Each party needs a certain amount of freedom from the other, which I was quite aware of

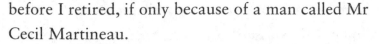

before I retired, if only because of a man called Mr Cecil Martineau.

Mr Cecil Martineau was a mandarin, or at least I think of him as such. He was the chief financial officer of the county, and a man of great power and influence which he exercised with elegance and dignity. He was tall and slim. He went to an expensive tailor, always wore the most admirable suits and for much of the year had a rose in his buttonhole. In those days most people smoked, as did he, and when he wanted a cigarette he would draw from his pocket a gold cigarette case and with long and tapering fingers select from it a Turkish cigarette. I think of him as a man of few words but of powerful effects.

Then he retired, and I came upon him later in a supermarket. He was following his wife around the store, pushing a trolley. All decisions as to what went into the trolley were taken by her and his duty was simply to trail behind and push the thing along. It struck me like a blow to the face to see this great man whom county councillors had treated with respect, for whose favour his colleagues used to compete and at whose word millions of pounds were spent in one way or another, now reduced to doing what was no more than the labour of an old-fashioned Chinese coolie.

I only saw him once after that, when I found him sitting patiently on a seat in a public library waiting for his wife to choose a book. 'Hello, Mr Martineau,' I said, and sat down beside him for a few minutes of conversation, although in earlier days I would not have dared to approach him so lightly. I brought him up to date, as well as I could, on the latest doings of the county council, this being the only topic we could have in common, and I felt he was positively grateful for this brief interlude in the normal routine of his existence.

For two to live in the same house with a reasonable degree of separation is easy enough, but there are those who go to quite unnecessary lengths to achieve it. Some couples have a car each, but we only have one, and this works perfectly well as I regard the car as something which belongs to my wife and not to me. My duty is to see that it is licensed, insured and serviced, and if I want to use it I fit in with her arrangements, which may sound difficult, but isn't. Some couples have two telephone lines, but we only

have one, with instruments all over the place. If I am in my study I let the phone ring five times before I pick it up, so that my wife can have first go at answering, and a question that I do not ask her is 'Who was that on the phone?' We treat the post in much the same way. We divide it between us but never say 'Who's that letter from?' In the normal way of things we almost always say who it was on the phone or what the letter was about, but this is at discretion. You may think that these are trivial matters, but a degree of shared privacy, so to speak, is what you need in such circumstances.

One of my successes has been to found an all-male luncheon group. I count it as a success as it has lasted for at least fifteen years, though with two changes of membership. There were four of us at the start, all of us for much of the time (and I speak with brutal frankness) stuck at home with our wives. We needed to get out for a bit of male conversation and while I do not know exactly what male conversation is, and although I could not define it with any accuracy, and in spite of the fact that I generally prefer the company of women, male conversation is a phenomenon which exists and of which one sometimes feels the need. We four agreed to meet for lunch at a pub on Wednesdays, which is what we did until one member moved away, and then with much care and deliberation we chose a substitute to fill his place. We declared, by mutual consent, that three should constitute a quorum, which meant that if two members could not come for any reason, there would be no meeting that week. If this happened it left such a gap in our lives that we thought it best to expand the membership to five. It took us several weeks to settle upon someone suitable to be dignified with an invitation, but eventually we hit upon the very man, and so, having now a membership of five and a quorum of three, it is rare that we do not assemble and meet together, as the Prayer Book puts it.

My wife has not formed any such group, but she goes to lunch with her friends without me, or has them to lunch with her when I am out of the way, which I presume must serve much the same purpose. These are both courses of action which I recommend.

I believe also that, if you look about you, you will find that there are ready-made groups which do much the same sort of thing. There is an organisation called Probus, and I have twice been asked to speak to Probus groups. The word *probus* in Latin means honest and upright, which I assumed was what they set out to be, but I was told that the word is coined to cover membership from PROfessional and BUSiness people. They get someone to give them a talk from time to time, as an excuse for a social gathering. I did not see any women in the audience on either occasion, so I suspect that in spite of the sex discrimination laws they have managed to make themselves an all male organisation, a sort of masculine Women's Institute, which is a very good thing for them to be.

Then there is the matter of holidays. You can go on holiday together, you can go with other people, you can join the children for a family holiday, you can go off with two other fellows like *Three Men in a Boat*, or you can go on holiday alone. In this matter I am exceptionally lucky, in that I have a liking for solitude and a wife who does not mind if I go off by myself. The other books I have written have all been about solitary trips made on a bicycle to one place and another, and when I go on one of these expeditions people evidently say to her 'Aren't you worried about him?' but she isn't. In truth, she is glad to have a rest from me.

In case you are tempted by the thought of a holiday on your own I will tell you briefly the pros and cons. In its favour is a complete lack of responsibility. You can do exactly what you like without any consultation or discussion, there being no one with whom to discuss and no one to consult. You can take risks and if they do not come off you have inconvenienced no one but yourself. If you spend an uncomfortable night in a disagreeable hotel you

have the comfort of knowing that you have not inflicted it on your wife. The writer William Hazlitt put it like this: 'One of the pleasantest things in the world is going on a journey, but I like to go by myself. The soul of a journey is liberty, perfect liberty, to think, feel, do, just as one pleases.'

The disadvantage is simply that you might not like it. A friend of ours who was rather taken with the sound of what I had been doing went travelling about northern Greece on his own and had a miserable time because he felt lonely. Others get lonely; I do not. It is a possibility of which I warn you.

Solitary travelling is much easier for men than for women, though I once, in Greece, met a German widow who was doing the same as I. We were seated at adjacent tables in a taverna at Preveza, each reading a book. I laughed at something in mine, she asked me what the joke was, and we got into conversation. We went for coffee together and then, I do assure you, she went to her hotel and I to mine. Next morning we met by agreement, took the bus together to Nicopolis, explored it together and I took another bus to Ioannina while she walked back to Preveza. We got on well, but never asked each other's names, so I have no idea who she was, or where she lived, or anything much about her. Our conversation was wholly on general topics but I remember that she said that on the Greek islands she was rather pestered by Greeks trying to pick her up, but not on the mainland, and that she had no other problems.

I have had other brief acquaintances with travellers who have turned up like this, and after a short time, moved off in a different direction from mine leaving me with a pleasant recollection of our meeting but without encumbering me with their company. This German lady, though, was the only woman among such brief acquaintances, but the most fearless traveller I know is one whom I have never met, a pen friend called Betty Lang. In her seventies and as deaf as anything, she leaves her husband behind and plunges into places I would hardly dare enter without an armed escort. It is all perfectly safe according to her, and she wrote a letter to the *Daily Mail* sticking up for the Balkans in general and saying, 'I am 73 and profoundly deaf, but I travel alone. This year, all I did was book a flight into Cilipi airport, Croatia, and armed with a Bradt travel guide and a large amount of euros tucked in my body belt, explored Montenegro. In 2005, 2006 and 2007 I did the same in Albania. I feel very safe in these Balkan countries – people help me, respect me and welcome me. I love to walk in lonely places and enjoy the peace and tranquillity I find, aided by my silent ears.' If she wrote to tell me she was about to explore Iraq or Afghanistan by bus and taxi I should not be a bit surprised.

On Sleep

'His only unhappiness proceeded from his
sleeping too little and thinking too much,
which sometimes threw him
into violent fevers.'

**Edward Hyde, Lord Clarendon (1607–1674),
writing of the theologian William Chillingworth**

One of the great pleasures of old age consists in sleeping after lunch. There are some who like twenty minutes, some half an hour, but I am a serious sleeper and can do with an hour or perhaps an hour and a quarter. To sleep for so long at such a time is, of course, a continental habit, and if it became general over here, it would be one of the few benefits to flow from our membership of the European Union. As it is, sleeping after lunch is only respectable if you are old, and it would be thought slothful, if not positively sinful, in a young person.

There is summer sleeping and winter sleeping. The best place to sleep after lunch on a fine summer's day is the garden, and it is worth parting with a little money to get one of those open-air beds they call a sun lounger. The moment when you have finished your lunch and uncoil yourself on a sun lounger in order to surrender yourself to sleep is one of the high spots of the day.

Given a fine spell of summer weather it is also possible to sleep in the garden by night, which is a pleasure of an altogether different sort. I discovered it more or less by accident, because we had a tent in which the children sometimes liked to sleep and when they were small I slept there with them, on an old army camp bed such as I used to have on my tank when trundling about Lüneburg Heath on some military exercise. (Officers, as I recall, slept on camp beds, and Other Ranks on the ground.) One day there was a great storm which blew the tent down and wrecked it, and this put paid to sleeping out for the children but not for me. On a hot fine night I took my camp bed and sleeping bag and went to bed under the stars at the place where the tent would have been if it hadn't been blown away. To do this, I can tell you, is a very fine experience. There you lie, flat on your back, gazing up into the universe, with the whole of infinity spread out before you, all sprinkled with stars. Eternity extends before you forever, and there is nothing like it to convince you of the smallness of the world, the tininess of man, and the insignificance of the minute part you have to play in the general order of things.

On a much humbler level, from sleeping in the garden I made an interesting discovery on my own account, which is that a hedgehog, when pressed, can run as fast as a greyhound. One moonlit night, as I lay on my camp bed a hedgehog appeared and started trundling about the garden. This had happened before, but on this particular night it coincided with my wife letting our greyhound out to do a wee. The dog came galloping up to say hello to me, and then spotted the hedgehog, which rather than doing what is supposed to be the proper thing and rolling itself into a ball and defying the dog from inside its prickles, ran away. They both flew across the garden, each of them going full tilt, and in a mad charge of about 30 yards the gap between the two did not narrow at all, and the hedgehog got to the safety of the hedge unharmed. I later mentioned this episode on some TV programme, which caused several viewers to write and say that I was talking utter nonsense, but one or two came to my support and testified from their own observation that when it comes to the 30-yard dash, the hedgehog is no slouch.

Sleeping at night, rather than by day, is a problem for some. My father used to say that he could sleep at any time and in any place except in bed at night. He used to take pills to send him to sleep, but these made him depressed, so he took tranquilisers to dispel the gloom, but they made him drowsy, so he took pep pills to counteract the tranquilisers. I think he would have done better to follow the advice of the late Bernard Levin, who used to write the same column once every ten years in which he said that all insomniacs should throw away their pills as the human body knows perfectly well how much sleep it needs, and will help itself to a little or a lot, as it feels necessary.

Dr William Enfield, my great-great-great-grandfather, wrote in a letter that 'Early rising is the secret of sleep in old age. I learnt this from Mr Wesley.' (He does not tell us which of the two Wesley brothers told him this.) I think there is a great deal in what he says. I sleep well, and am an early riser by inclination, getting up at about 6.30 a.m. in winter, and perhaps earlier in summer. To drink a cup of tea in the early morning is a very pleasant thing, and I find the first hour of the day a productive time for reading or writing, as well as an aid to sleep later on.

My neighbour once had a very fine chestnut horse on which he used to hunt, and the groom told me that after a day's hunting the horse always re-lived it all in his box at night, stamping and whinnying and trembling as he went over the whole day time and time again. The same thing can happen to us, and it stops you going to sleep. If you are troubled that way, my suggestion is that you learn the names and dates of the kings and queens of England, and recite them to yourself in bed. I find that, starting from William the Conqueror I am often asleep by Henry II, rarely get beyond Edward V, occasionally manage the Tudors and even the Stuarts but hardly ever reach the Hanoverians. Very occasionally I get right through to Elizabeth II, so then I start on the early Roman emperors, and they knock me out altogether. I suggest that you try this, and even if it does not send you to sleep, you will at least be better informed on the general structure of English history and possibly of the history of Rome as well.

On Gardening

'The Emperor Diocletian, when pressed by Maximian to resume power, rejected the temptation with a smile of pity, calmly observing that if he could show Maximian the cabbages which he had planted with his own hands at Salona, he should no longer be urged to relinquish the enjoyment of happiness for the pursuit of power.'

Edward Gibbon (1737–1794),
The Decline and Fall of the Roman Empire

Old people always have gardens if they possibly can. We live near the town of Petworth, where once a year fifteen or so gardens are open to the public for some charitable purpose. When you visit, you go from one set of old people to the next, all of whom have been labouring with tremendous energy to get their gardens into tip-top shape for the occasion. They do this because one of the principal pleasures of gardeners is to show off their gardens to other people. They don't seem to feel like this about the inside of their houses, but they do about the outside. Even if your elderly friends have no more than a little courtyard or patio, although you can pass through the living room without making any comment, when you arrive at the patio you are to praise the beauty of the geraniums and the healthy state of the potted plants. You may find that you are invited for coffee at short notice on a fine day, as a thinly disguised recruitment drive to find people to admire the garden.

This is a most innocent foible, and if the roses are looking well I can feel the temptation to do the same, but I resist it. I do not garden to the standard of those who open their gardens to the public, if only because that would mean allowing the garden to take over my life, which it would if I let it. In fact, one of my two principles of gardening is to stop this happening, and as we

have a garden of about three quarters of an acre,
it takes a bit of doing.

The solution so far has been to turn a large part
of it into a chicken run, with wire netting to keep
the birds in and an electric fence to keep the fox
out. All I have to do is keep the electric fence clear
of weeds and mow the grass from time to time. The
chickens themselves do quite a lot towards keeping

the grass down, and the rest is easy enough as I have a first rate self-propelled mower which does the job in no time. Beyond the chicken run things become more complicated.

Part of the garden is vegetable bed, and as I started originally from a basis of complete ignorance I bought, in about 1960, a book by Lawrence D. Hills called *Down to Earth Fruit and Vegetable Growing*. Lawrence Hills is the founder and patron saint of the organic gardening movement, and as my copy of his book is the first edition, complete with dust jacket and 'not price clipped', as booksellers put it, it might have a certain value if I had not written a lot of notes on the blank pages at the back. It struck me when I bought it that it was an odd sort of book, and after this lapse of time it seems odder than ever. It tells you that 'the favourite food of rhubarb is wool shoddy, and an old flock mattress will provide plenty'. According to L. D. Hills you could easily buy such a mattress from a second-hand furniture shop, but I don't believe that this was at all easy then, and it certainly isn't now. Again, if you are troubled with insects, he tells you to make your own nicotine insecticide by boiling 4 ounces of cigarette ends in 2 gallons of water with a pound of soft soap, which may be a frightfully organic idea but is not, in my view, practical. However, large parts of the book make perfect sense and, starting from this, while I have had my ups and downs over the years I can generally persuade the vegetable bed to produce a reasonable selection of beans and green stuff and some tolerable fruit.

Beyond that there is lawn, there are hedges, there are flower beds, and with the passage of time this is bound to be more than we can manage (my wife's role being chiefly to deadhead the roses and the dahlias). The answer to this coming difficulty has been provided by my eighty-four-year-old widowed sister, whose garden is just as big as ours but gives her almost no trouble. She has contracted out the hedge and grass cutting and leaves the beds to look after themselves. Hers is, she says, a garden run on the Darwinian principle of the survival of the fittest, and the last time I saw it the lawn was trim, the trees and shrubs were flourishing, and along the edges some stout-hearted day lilies, unconquerable phloxes and determined roses were slugging it out with cover provided by a carpet of ground elder. It all looked splendid, and provided what I regard as the ideal solution to the gardening problem.

I have spoken of my two principles of gardening, and the second I learnt from a slow, loquacious Welshman whose name was Pryce. It was in the days when I was working for a rapacious Swiss chemical firm called Ciba, which has since merged with some other equally rapacious Swiss firms to create a combination called Novartis. At the time I speak of, my particular part of the whole Ciba organisation had been devoted to fleecing the National Health Service of every penny that could be got and exporting the resultant profits to Switzerland without paying tax. Then it was decided to branch out into agricultural chemicals, and it was thought that in order to experiment with the newly invented chemicals which were supposed to come flowing in from Basle, a farm would be needed. Accordingly, the management hurried out and bought the first farm that came on the market within a reasonable distance of the main factory. Having now got a farm, they felt the need for a farm manager and instead of advertising for such a person, and getting someone who knew a bit about it to help them choose, they looked about them and found that they had a sometime farm manager working as a storeman. This was the slow, loquacious Pryce who was immediately uplifted out of the stores and installed as manager of the farm. Above him was put a young agricultural graduate called Alf Lewis, who was to arrange the experiments and see to the running of the farm. Generally, Alf Lewis was an impatient man, and was constantly trying to hurry Pryce along, while Pryce was as constantly determined to go at his own leisurely pace. Alf Lewis was also a big man, and something of a bully, and if Pryce had weakened his life would have been a misery, but every time Alf tried to set him in motion, Pryce would mount a leisurely defence punctuated by meditative pauses. It went like this:

'When I was a young man, Mr Lewis, I was just the same as you. Always in a hurry. Just like you, Mr Lewis. Always wanting to get on, the same as you, Mr Lewis.'

At this point Pryce would indulge in one of his pauses, but if Alf Lewis tried to speak, he immediately started again:

'I used to worry, Mr Lewis. Gave myself ulcers worrying, I did. Then I learnt, Mr Lewis, that you cannot hurry Nature.' A further pause here ensued, before the final punch line:

'You have to wait for Nature, Mr Lewis – you cannot hurry Nature.'

One of Pryce's subtleties was to ignore the fact that Alf Lewis had a PhD and liked to be called Dr Lewis. By constantly calling him Mr Lewis and by stubbornly resisting the idea of getting on, he used regularly to reduce Alf Lewis to a frenzy.

I admired Pryce for this, and I often think of him in the context of our garden, of which the soil is very heavy clay, absorbing compost, farmyard manure or lime without any alteration to its essential nature. At two extremes it either sets into an impenetrable rock or it resolves itself into a sticky, waterlogged porridge. If you want to do any cultivation you must catch it on the hop as it passes from one state to the other and for this, as Pryce remarked, you have to wait for Nature. This, therefore, is the second of my principles of gardening – not to give myself ulcers by trying to hurry Nature.

On Old Age and
the Bicycle

'Bicycling down the face of a mountain, over curves that take you half a mile or a mile in one direction, and then as far in the other direction, is about the nearest approach to flying that has yet been given to man.'

Rufus B. Richardson, *Vacation Days in Greece*

From time to time I see, on the little road which runs past our house, some foolish old man, and occasionally some foolish old woman, jogging. Bang bang bang go their poor old feet on the hard tarmac surface, jarring their spines, damaging their knees and preparing their hips for the day when they have to be rebuilt in plastic. 'Why on earth,' say I to myself, 'don't you get yourselves bicycles?'

I have never done anything so foolish as to go jogging, but I can say with certainty that it is unpleasant. It is not just that this is obvious from the look on the faces of the joggers; at one time I had some experience of long distance running, which is certainly unpleasant, and undoubtedly similar. I was just good enough to be the last boy picked for the school cross-country team and in any race I always trailed in after everyone else, having resisted the temptation to lie down in the ditch and pretend I had sprained an ankle – a temptation which always came upon me when the pain was at its highest. I do not suppose that jogging is quite as bad as that, and I am not going to try to find out, but I can see that the symptoms are similar and it is clearly an unpleasant, as well as potentially harmful, way of trying to do yourself good.

Anything that can be got from jogging can be got from cycling. If it is pain you are after, you can cycle fast into a headwind. If you want to set your heart pumping, ride up a steep hill. If you want to

fill your lungs with fresh air, stretch the muscles of your legs and burn up a quantity of calories, a bicycle is the place to do it, because there it can be done not just without unpleasantness, but with positive pleasure. To ride along a quiet country road with the tyres gently hissing beneath you, to catch a whiff of honeysuckle here and there, to hear the song of birds or the sounds of cattle, to look out over fields or orchards towards distant hills – if you were a triple multi-millionaire on your yacht in the Bahamas you could not get anything as good as that, and it need cost you almost nothing.

Of course, if you live in a big city it is not so easy, as pedalling through traffic is not much fun and carries with it the danger of being killed. All the same, if you can find somewhere reasonable to ride, cycling conveys a benefit which I have never seen described, though other cyclists have found the same. It is, in brief, good for the mind. If you are feeling generally dissatisfied, out of sorts, unusually grumpy or anything else along these lines, go for a bicycle ride and the feeling will be dispelled, to be replaced by one of contentment, bonhomie and general well-being. I discovered this when I was a boy in Canada and I re-discovered it in later life. If this phenomenon were more generally known, doctors would prescribe cycling as a treatment for depression, anxiety, melancholia, hypochondria and sundry other diseases of the mind, to the great benefit of their patients and probably with a great saving to the health service on tranquilisers, anti-depressants and other drugs of that nature.

If you do not have a bicycle but are tempted by what I have written, there is no need to go rushing into vast expenditure. While a very good new bicycle can be bought for well under £300, a perfectly adequate second-hand one can be found for about £20 from some local paper. In my late fifties, having had no bicycle for many years, I bought for £15 a 3-speed model which I rode to Rouen and back with my wife. This was such a pleasant experience that I later bought a superior new Dawes and have cycled vigorously ever since. You, if you approach it in this way, should not start with some fancy racing machine with complicated gears, but with a sturdy touring model which has the gear change on the handlebars. After that there is no saying what may happen. In the course of time you may find yourself flashing about country lanes wearing a Lycra leotard, a form of dress which I avoid but which many seem to go in for.

I was lucky enough to retire at the age of sixty-two. I mentioned in an earlier chapter that my colleagues gave me a tent as a leaving present, and one of my first acts in retirement was to put it on the back of my lovely new Dawes and cycle from the Channel to the Mediterranean. I went hopping from campsite to campsite, I was away for a month, and I had an altogether delightful time. Since then I have cycled in Greece, Ireland, Germany, Poland and Austria, and I tell you that not because I suppose you are in the least interested in my activities, but to illustrate the sort of things a bicycle will enable you to do, and to show that old age is no bar to mild adventures on a bicycle.

On Not Doing
It Yourself

Lord Macaulay 'was unhandy to a degree quite unexampled in the experience of all who knew him. He hurt his hand, and was reduced to send for a barber. After the operation he asked what was to pay. "Oh, Sir," said the man, "whatever you give the man who usually shaves you." "In that case," said Macaulay, "I should give you a great gash on each cheek."'

G. O. Trevelyan (1809–1859),
Life and Letters of Lord Macaulay

We bought our house in 1960 and have lived here ever since. Although I am the least handy of handymen there cannot be an inside wall that I have not, at some time, painted or papered, nor yet a window frame that I have not rubbed with sandpaper or coated with paint stripper. In my early enthusiasm I bought an electric drill which had all sorts of gadgets to go with it, such as one that was supposed to remove paint from wood, but did not. I made some rudimentary attempts at carpentry and a botched endeavour at brick building, in the form of a precarious and short-lived coal bunker. All this, I am pleased to say, is now behind me, though my legs still ache at the thought of the hours I spent teetering on the narrow rungs of a long wooden ladder.

There are men, and I suppose in this enlightened age there may be women, to whom such things are as the breath of life. They delight in workshops with racks of shiny tools, they buy all the latest bits of equipment, and provide themselves with strange things such as trolley jacks. They tear their kitchens to pieces and put them together again in a new form. They grapple hand to hand with plumbing and are quite fearless in their approach to electricity. If this is their hobby, then by all means they must indulge in it, even into old age, but for those of us who would rather not, there are ample reasons why we shouldn't.

I pass over the fact that such activities deprive decent tradesmen of sundry chances to earn an honest living, and go straight to the fact that this thing called DIY is dangerous. As long ago as the year 2000 I made a note that the government had discovered that seventy people were being killed every year, and a quarter of a million injured, as a result of Doing It Themselves. Government statistics said so. The then Minister for Consumer Affairs, Mr Kim Howell, issued a special warning against the screwdriver. 'People are always puncturing themselves with screwdrivers,' he said, and I shuddered to think how often I had taken in hand a screwdriver, even the pointed version called a Phillips, without giving the least thought to the possibility of my puncturing myself. As for the stepladder! 'A survey for the DTI,' said one of his officials, 'found that the average consumer was unable to detect more than half of the eleven dangers which can result from using stepladders.' I could see that I might fall off such a ladder, and

that it might fall over, and that it might somehow collapse altogether, but I could not think of a single one of the other eight dangers, which shows that I am not even an average consumer but a hopelessly sub-average one.

I detected, at that time, a move against Doing It Yourself. I read in the paper that: 'Many people are so busy that they have to hire other people to do their DIY.' The idea of hiring someone else to Do It Yourself is a difficult logical concept. It may be existential (a word of whose meaning I am never sure) or even border upon the metaphysical, but all the same it is perfectly sound. I wondered if I could get some newspaper to commission me to write a regular column, headed 'Don't Do It Yourself'. I envisaged lively articles on such subjects as Septicaemia and the Screwdriver, Perils of the Power Tool, and Easier than Falling Off a Ladder. Nobody seemed very keen on the idea, but never mind. In our younger days we all had to Do It Ourselves, as we could not afford not to, but now we are of riper years we can, I hope, hire someone else to Do It For Us. In my case I model myself on the centurion in the Bible – he whom I have mentioned before – and say to the painter 'Paint!' and he painteth, and to the plumber 'Plumb!' and he plumbeth, and to the carpenter 'Fix it!' and he fixeth it. I find this to be very restful, and I recommend it.

On Death

'Pass through this little space of time and
end thy journey in content, just as an olive
falls off when it is ripe, blessing nature
which produced it, and thanking the
tree on which it grew.'

Marcus Aurelius

If I said that death usually gets a bad press this
would not be an original idea because I stole
it from Damon Runyon, that great American
writer who created all the characters of *Guys and
Dolls*. Death came to visit him in hospital, most
nattily dressed in a white flannel suit. This, Death

explained, was part of his campaign to give a cheerful impression of himself, as he was gloomily aware that he was by no means generally popular. He asked Runyon if he could ever become, as he put it, 'a social success', but Runyon was not encouraging. In desperation, Death revealed that he had thought of hiring a firm of public relations consultants to polish up his image. Did Runyon think that this would work?

'It might,' said Runyon. 'The publicity men have worked wonders with even worse cases than yours.' We tend nowadays to shy away from the subject of death, unless it is murder, and then the papers

revel in it. The Greeks and Romans used to talk about it a lot. 'True philosophers,' said Socrates, 'give a lot of thought to death. It is less alarming to them than to anyone else.' Cicero says firmly that if he was offered the chance of starting life all over again he would turn it down. 'If some god were generously to offer that I might, from my present age, revert to being a baby wailing in my cradle, I should stoutly refuse. Having run the race, I would not like to go back again from the finishing post to the starting line.' I agree with Cicero in this. I shouldn't like to go round again with everything happening as it happened before – the good and the bad, the same successes and failures, the same hopes and disappointments. Although I have been very fortunate in life so far, I agree with Cicero's view of the matter.

My father-in-law took a great interest in obituaries. My mother-in-law was called Poppy but he always called her Pops, and from time to time he would peer over the top of his newspaper and say, 'Good God, Pops – there's another one gone!' Then he would gleefully read out the obituary of someone they had known some years before. I share this taste. I get a magazine from my old school, and another from my old college, and yet another from the regiment in which I did my national service. Whenever one arrives I turn at once to the obituaries to see if I have managed to outlive any of my contemporaries. I have to confess that I am always rather disappointed if there is no one in the list whom I remember, and I am even slightly cheered if there is another one gone. When my own name appears, I expect that others will feel the same.

Attitudes to death have altered a lot in my lifetime. When I was a schoolboy we used regularly, as part of school prayers, to go through the litany in the Book of Common Prayer. The headmaster would declaim the words, 'From all evil and mischief; from sin, from the craft and assaults of the devil; from thy wrath, and from everlasting damnation,' to which we would reply with one voice, 'Good Lord, deliver us.' When these words were first written people must have thought it necessary that they should be constantly on their guard against the craft of the devil, and have the possibility of everlasting damnation kept in the forefront of their minds, and I suppose they still thought this in the 1940s when I was at school.

We also used to say, as part of the same process and with equal enthusiasm, '... from battle and murder, and from sudden death, Good Lord, deliver us.' Most of us old fellows nowadays would have no objection to sudden death, as one of our few remaining desires is to get out of the world without having a horrid time and without being a beastly nuisance. The lucky ones are those that drop dead at a moment's notice, but it used to be thought that you needed a chance to settle your affairs with the Almighty before you went. Hamlet's father, for example, complained most bitterly at having been, as he said,

'Sent to my account
With all my imperfections on my head.'

As far as I know the evidence for or against such ideas has not altered since my schooldays, but people have just stopped worrying about the devil and damnation, which is certainly more comfortable, and I hope they are right.

Apart from any spiritual steps which you may think necessary, it is very important that you make a will. The father of some friends of mine caused them untold trouble by leaving lots of money but no will, as it took them at least ten years to get the estate settled. Let me now warn you, with all possible solemnity, that when you make a will you must not appoint either a solicitor or a bank as your executor. The solicitor who draws up your will may suggest such an idea, and your bank may issue you with a persuasive leaflet on this subject, but be guided by me and have none of it. If you have already taken this ill-advised step, then you should somehow get rid of the solicitor, or the bank, as the case may be, by making a new will or perhaps by codicil if this will do the trick.

I learned the dangers of having a solicitor as an executor from a friend whose aunt had appointed such a one. Cheating, shuffling, lying, over-charging, procrastinating and battening on the estate less like a leech than a vampire were the chief features of this man's executorship. My friend found out by bitter experience that the only people who can remove executors from wills are the people who put them in, i.e. the testators, and if they are dead at the time it is too late. In despair my friend applied to the

Law Society and found that their system is clogged up with hundreds of complaints about reprobate solicitors, which they are dealing with in the usual leisurely lawyer-like manner, so there is a good chance that the heirs will themselves be dead before the matter is settled.

Of course, you may have appointed a solicitor in whom you have absolute trust, on the excellent grounds that you and he were at school together or that you play golf with her father. Bear in mind, though, that solicitors have the same frailties as the rest of us, and do such things as pre-decease their clients, become senile or go to jail. In such cases some other member of the firm may arise and take over and he or she may well be useless, or evil, or both. If you make your wife and your daughter or your son and your brother your executors, you have done the right thing, because they can hire a lawyer when they need one and fire him if he turns out to be evil, but if you make a lawyer your executor your heirs will be stuck with him come what may.

As for banks, I found when my uncle died that banks do nothing and charge a lot for doing it. You might think that the executor divisions of banks would have lawyers to do legal work and valuers to do valuations, but they haven't. They just hire outside lawyers and valuers, pay their fees and pile their own fees on top, helping themselves freely from your money out of the estate.

You might perhaps think I have been a little hard on lawyers, but I have come to the conclusion that for peace of mind in many aspects of life it is a good idea to keep out of the clutches of lawyers, and also banks, if you possibly can. Let me quote to you (from memory as I cannot trace the original) a letter from the painter Thomas Gainsborough which he wrote to an attorney whom he had recently met: 'I am sorry that I said not one lawyer in ten was worth the trouble of hanging but I did not realise at the time that you was one. The truth is that I never met a man of your profession with such an honest countenance, which is why I concluded that you must be in the wool trade.'

So much for lawyers. As well as your will there is also the matter of your funeral, about which it is probably helpful to leave a few directions. In my case I will say that I am not keen on readings from best-selling Indian mystics (which is what some people go in for) or of bits of poetry from here and there. I would like to have as much of the funeral service from the old Book of Common Prayer as seems reasonable, including Psalm 103, Verses 8–18, with the words:

> The days of man are but as grass: for he flourisheth like a flower of the field. For as soon as the wind goeth over it, it is gone: and the place thereof shall know it no more.

If there is to be an address, I ask that it be kept short, lasting not more than seven minutes. I am an Old Boy of Westminster School, and if I may be allowed three hymns I would like them to have been written by other Old Westminsters. I should like to have 'God Moves in a Mysterious Way' (William Cowper), 'Love Divine All Loves Excelling' (Charles Wesley) and 'As Pants the Heart for Cooling Stream' (Nahum Tate and Nicholas Brady, of whom only Brady was an Old Westminster). That sounds a good sort of service to me, and I am only sorry that I shan't be there in person.

On Ambition

'Old people like to have everything calm and orderly, as for them it is too late for hard work, and ambition would be undignified.'

Pliny the Younger

Pliny speaks of hard work, and I can honestly say that it is a great many years since I have done anything that could be so described. I recently got a load of horse manure for the flowerbeds and spent a morning industriously shovelling and busily barrowing the stuff, but I don't count that as hard work. It does not compare with the fearful fag of bringing home a briefcase stuffed with papers and wasting part of the weekend in dictating to a machine. Still less does it compare with the sort of thing that goes on in the City of London, where I never worked but where I had a source in the shape of a young lady who managed a sandwich bar. She told me her customers were yobs and hooligans who worked terribly hard, were terribly stressed, and in those days used to get terribly rich. Having a great deal of money but little time to spend it, they got drunk and went to lap dancing clubs as a way of getting rid of some of it. Compare that with the calm and orderly life that Pliny speaks of and you can see how lucky we old people are.

I certainly like to have things orderly and, while I must be careful what I say, I am always pleased when I look at my diary and find that nothing is happening. Glad as I am to see the people who come to visit us, and delighted as I am to visit the people we go to see, it is a very nice thing to have a day which falls into a tidy pattern in which nothing is going on.

As for ambition, it is a lovely thing to be without. One of the great comforts of old age is that you can look back with satisfaction on such things as you may have achieved, while you have come to terms with your failures, which no longer matter. It may be, perhaps, that you went into the army hoping to become a general and were eventually pensioned off with the rank of major. There is nothing to be done about it, and there are bound to be many aspects of your army life that make you feel good in retrospect when you look back upon them. I can speak only of the two years I spent in the army, during which time I was a dreadful failure as an officer, but in spite of that I can reflect with great pleasure on the episode as a whole. I remember the freezing cold of the barrack huts at Catterick Camp with something like affection, and I have the fondest memories of all the horses and many of the officers of the regiment in which I served. I think often of my now deceased squadron leader, Richard Dill, who once introduced me as 'one of my least efficient troop leaders', this being a classic case of the true word spoken in jest, and I have no grudge against those other subalterns who were much more efficient than I.

It is probably more likely that you went into business rather than the army, hoping to become a managing director, if not a chairman, and ended up as something humbler like an assistant sales manager or a deputy company secretary. Never mind; now that you are no longer trying to climb the ladder of success you are not threatened by the sort of person who hangs about the water cooler hoping to pour poison into the ear of the managing director. If you have any doubts as to how lucky you are to be out of it all, have a look at the Appointments section of the newspaper. 'Are you a self-starter?' asks one advertisement. 'You need to be a self-starter,' says another. I put it to you, did anyone ever ask you such a silly question or make such a silly statement, and could you bear to be in a world where they evidently do?

Imagine yourself going for an interview and trying to pass yourself off as 'hungry for the challenge of Procurement Transformation on a grand scale' or trying to persuade a group of people that you are 'an evangelist with skills in driving direct response mechanisms in a niche market'. It is all too horrible to contemplate, especially as by entering one of these organisations you would cease to be a person and become a Human Resource, an idea I have always thought to be particularly insulting. Of course, it may all be a hoax, and evangelists hungry for challenge may exist only in the imagination of recruitment consultants and people who write advertisements. I find it difficult to believe that if young Bobby says to his father, 'What do you do at your office, daddy?', the answer he gets is, 'I deliver truly innovative and business-focused HR policies.' Nor can I suppose that when people go out on dates the conversation goes like this:

Jennifer: Tell me, Edward – I have long been wondering, are you a self-starter?

Edward: My dear Jennifer, let me assure you that I have a proven track record of self-starting, not to mention owning and shaping new products and programs to produce results.

Jennifer: Wow!

No, it cannot be as bad as that, but even if it is a little bit like that, it is a tremendous relief to be out of a world where people can even bring themselves to pretend that such is the way of things.

On the Arts

'I do not think altogether the worse of
a book for having survived the author a
generation or two. I have more confidence
in the dead than the living.'

William Hazlitt (1778–1830)

If you want to see old people out in force, go to a matinee of something like a Gilbert and Sullivan operetta at somewhere like the Chichester Festival Theatre. We went, a few years ago, to exactly that – a Carla Rosa production of *The Pirates of Penzance* at that very theatre at two in the afternoon. The elderly came in droves. They not only filled the

ample theatre car park, but they overflowed into all the nearby parks as well and I had to abandon our car on a patch of grass where it had no business to be, narrowly escaping a fine. One charabanc after another slowly set down its aged cargo as close to the theatre as possible, so that the elderly patrons had not far to hobble to the entrance. We, being but in our early seventies, must have brought the average age down by a fraction of a decimal point, and when drinking coffee beforehand felt obliged to jump up and offer our seats in the foyer to others older than ourselves. It was one of the most delightful experiences of my life. I like Gilbert and Sullivan, the performance was well done, and I warmed to the audience as well as to the performers because everyone enjoyed it so much.

The old go in for the arts like anything. They go to plays and concerts, they shuffle about in art galleries, they read no end of a lot of books and they enrol upon Open University courses and become enlightened about the Enlightenment. They join NADFAS, the National Association of Decorative and Fine Arts Societies, and if you see a group of earnest elderly women with a couple of obedient-

looking men emerging from a bus in somewhere like
Norwich, it is probably a branch of NADFAS come
to see the pictures in the Norwich Castle Museum.
They do all this because they have leisure for such
things and their tastes are properly developed. The
young, by contrast, having juvenile tastes, flock
to hear stand-up comedians making coarse jokes
which no mature person would ever laugh at.

I myself am an occasional theatre goer, rather
than a regular one. It takes a good play to take my
mind off the actors, who all too often are not much
good at acting and by their prancing about on the

stage distract me from what is meant to be going on. I suffered like that with Laurence Olivier, who seemed to me to be a perfectly rotten tragic actor, given to bellowing and flinging himself about, but a brilliant comic actor. I realised this from seeing him on a double bill which started with the *Oedipus Rex* of Sophocles in which he was quite awful, followed by *The Critic*, a little play by Sheridan, in which he was so extremely funny that the whole theatre was in an uproar of laughter. One purpose in going to the theatre is to stock one's mind with recollections of such things. As Lord Byron remarked, 'The past at least is one's own, which is one reason for making sure of the present.'

When it comes to music I am simply inadequate and have no useful guidance to offer. The modern world expects school children to be able to read, write and do sums, all of which I can manage well enough, but if, like the Greeks, they put great stress on musical ability, I should have been classed as seriously handicapped and consigned to a school for the musically dyslexic. It is not that I am tone deaf – I can tell 'The British Grenadiers' from 'Men of Harlech' – but I cannot sing a note and the only attempt made at teaching me the piano was a hopeless failure.

Lack of ability is not necessarily a barrier to advancement in the world of music. This I discovered when I was talking to the bandmaster of the Eighth Hussars, the regiment in which I did my national service. In those days every regiment had a band, and the band's duty was to play marches on ceremonial occasions and to play music to officers on regimental dinner nights. Cavalry officers love dressing up, and on mess nights we came into the mess wearing tight trousers called overalls and patent leather boots called wellingtons, with chain mail clinking on our shoulders and spurs rattling on our heels. The long mahogany table glistened with regimental silver in the form of race cups and statuettes, and there we sat, chatting and drinking and clinking our spurs, while the band played in an ante-room.

It was on one of these occasions that I was talking to the bandmaster, whose name was something like Flew. He had the rank of staff sergeant and so was to be addressed as 'Mr Flew'. Our conversation went like this:

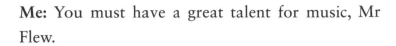

Me: You must have a great talent for music, Mr Flew.

Mr Flew: No. Very little.

Me: Come now, Mr Flew, this is carrying modesty too far. A man does not rise to be bandmaster of a distinguished regiment without a great deal of musical ability.

Mr Flew: I was recruited into the army as a band boy. They taught me to read music and play the clarinet and that is all I did.

Me: There you are! You play the clarinet – no doubt very well.

Mr Flew: Not really. I could read the notes on the sheet of music and I could blow them in the order in which they came so that is what I did.

To Mr Flew, it seems, music was a sort of exercise in military drill with the notes like a series of orders to be played in due sequence in a smart and soldierlike manner. Perhaps most bandsmen are like this. Anyway, nobody found any fault in the band of the Eighth Hussars, but if I had the misfortune to be recruited into the army as a band boy I think it most unlikely that I would have made such a success of it as did Mr Flew.

My wife is not musically handicapped, and so we go to concerts and similar performances from time to time, including, once, to the opera at Glyndebourne. The audience, as I recall, was mostly elderly and probably mostly rich, as the tickets are very expensive. The opera was *The Marriage of Figaro*, and the conductor Sir Simon Rattle, who seemed to conduct at very great speed. I remember the occasion chiefly for a conversation I had with another old fellow whom I met in the interval.

'The conductor,' said I, 'seems to be taking us through this at racing pace.'

'That's nothing,' he replied. 'Last night he knocked ten minutes off the record for *Don Giovanni*. The fellow's not called Rattle for nothin', you know.'

As for pictures, I can certainly give you a useful tip which I got from a newspaper many years ago. It is: 'Do not look at pictures for more than an hour together, because after that you will cease to take them in.'

This will be a great comfort to you if you happen to find yourself at a gallery in somewhere like Siena, faced with several hundred yards of Old Masters, or in Paris with a complete railway station stuffed with Impressionists. To take the case of Siena, an hour is quite enough to give to Holy Families (looking as the holy family never looked), to St Sebastian (looking like a pincushion), and to biblical and mythological scenes which make you feel inadequate because you do not understand the biblical reference or know the classical myth. After an hour it all becomes a blur and your legs get tired, so you had better go away and have a rest, which you can do with a perfectly clear conscience once you have put in an hour.

I recently read an essay by William Hazlitt in which he said that the Dulwich Gallery has 356 pictures. Assuming that it has the same number now as when he wrote in 1823, if one rounds 356 up to 360, a quick calculation shows that if you gave not one, but two hours to a visit and tried to see all the pictures you would devote twenty seconds to each one without allowing time for moving from picture to picture or from room to room. We have never been to Dulwich, but mean to go one day, and when we do I shall resolutely pass straight by a great many works by supreme masters of painting in order to concentrate on a few pictures that I most like the look of.

Then there are books, and here I have a suggestion to put before you. There is a small number of books about which everyone knows something but which by no means everyone has read. For a start, everybody has some idea of *Gulliver's Travels*, *The Strange Case of Dr Jekyll and Mr Hyde*, *Uncle Tom's Cabin*, *Robinson Crusoe* and *Tom Brown's Schooldays*, but such idea as they have may be sketchy, inadequate and even positively wrong. I remember Max Hastings, sometime editor of *The Daily Telegraph* and author of many books, writing about *Tom Brown's Schooldays* as if he had read it when he most obviously hadn't. He said of Dr Arnold, the great headmaster of Rugby, that 'Arnold and his contemporaries increased pupils' woes by encouraging the view that being roasted over a fire by Flashman represented a fulfilment of the divine will.' This, I am sorry to say, is utter nonsense, and possibly blasphemous nonsense at that. In *Tom Brown's Schooldays*, Tom does indeed get roasted by Flashman but, so far from encouraging such things, Dr Arnold's views on bullying were the exact opposite of what Mr Hastings supposes, and if he had read the book before basing his opinion on it he would have saved himself from a blunder unbecoming in an eminent historian.

But that is by the way, and the mistake is not one you are likely to make unless you happen to be a journalist. My point is that these books have established themselves as part of the background to modern life and possibly you might like to find out why, if you have not read them all already. I do not say the list is complete, and indeed I find that it sprouts another book from time to time. The word 'Kafkaesque' is freely bandied about, but it was a point of honour with me not to use it as I had never read any of Kafka's novels. Then I read *The Trial* and I can now, with a clear conscience, describe the planning department of Horsham District Council as Kafkaesque; this being the council in whose area we live and whose planners treated some friends of ours in the impenetrably mysterious and malevolently oppressive manner to which the word applies.

I do not want to set you a task of wading through my list of books, whether you like them or not, as a form of homework to be got through when you would rather read a thriller from the public library. Quite the reverse. Whether or not you fancy reading the standard works that I have suggested, I would say that you should not bother to finish any book you are not enjoying unless it is about some subject on which you feel the need to be better informed. Otherwise, whatever the book may be, if you have not taken kindly to it after a chapter or two, give it up, as there are hundreds and hundreds more out there waiting for you to try them and, at our age, time may be running out.

For this reason I very rarely get beyond a few pages of any modern novel unless it is written by John Grisham. In Jane Austen's *Northanger Abbey* there is a character called John Thorpe who says, 'Novels are all so full of nonsense and stuff; there has not been a tolerable one come out since *Tom Jones*.' That is going back rather far, but if one substitutes Evelyn Waugh's *Sword of Honour* for *Tom Jones*, I

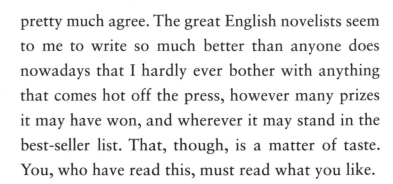

pretty much agree. The great English novelists seem to me to write so much better than anyone does nowadays that I hardly ever bother with anything that comes hot off the press, however many prizes it may have won, and wherever it may stand in the best-seller list. That, though, is a matter of taste. You, who have read this, must read what you like.

EDWARD ENFIELD

GREECE
ON MY WHEELS

FOREWORD BY HARRY ENFIELD

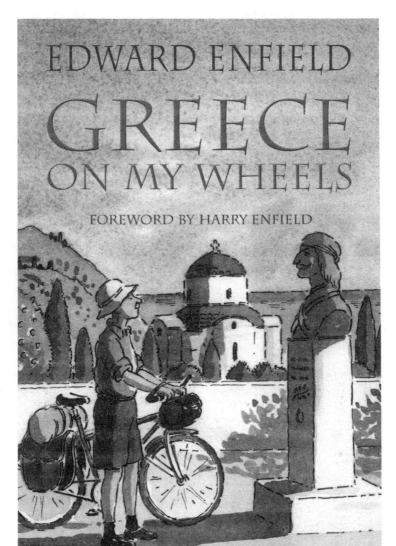

GREECE ON MY WHEELS

Edward Enfield

ISBN: 978 1 84024 280 5   Paperback   £8.99

Fired by a long enthusiasm for all things Greek, Edward Enfield mounts his trusty Raleigh to follow in the footsteps of such notable travellers to Greece as Benjamin Disraeli, Edward Lear and the Romantic poet Lord Byron.

Fortified by delicious fish dinners and quantities of draught retsina, he tackles the formidable roads of the Peloponnese before plunging, on a later trip, into the rugged heartlands of Epirus and Acarnania. His travels are set against the great panorama of Greek history – Greeks and Romans, Turks and Albanians, Venetians, Englishmen and Germans all people his pages.

An enchanting travelogue that combines wit, charm and scholarship, *Greece On My Wheels* is a superb example of travel writing at its unforgettable best.

Edward Enfield is a well-known television presenter. *Greece On My Wheels* is his second book.

'I would not have expected an account of one man's travels around Greece on a bicycle to be such fun. This is so much more than a travelogue... It is a delightful introduction to a wonderful country, and a story well told'
Saga TRAVELLERS NEWS

'Enfield not only impresses – he informs and delights... the overall effect is charming... it will give you a bit of knowledge and a warm glow' WANDERLUST

'Full of humour and wonderful depictions of the wild beauty and fascinating people of Greece – all seen from the saddle of his trusty steed' THE OLDIE

Have you enjoyed this book?
If so, why not write a review
on your favourite website?

Thanks very much for buying
this Summersdale book.

www.summersdale.com